C000001506

80 YEARS OF GUY MOTORS
1914-1994

For details of other transport titles available from Venture Publications Ltd please send a stamped addressed envelope to PO Box 17 Glossop SK13 9FA

Front Cover Illustration

Guy's post-war passenger production was based on the Arab which had proved its worth during the war in many fleets where Guys had not previously featured, or where only odd examples had been operated. Lancashire United Transport of Atherton was a good example, building up a large fleet of various Guy models and this Arab V with Northern Counties forward-entrance bodywork has been preserved and now resides in the Manchester Museum of Transport. It is seen operating at a Halifax rally in May 1994.
Photo J. A. Senior

Typeset and produced electronically for the Publishers by
Mopok Graphics, 128, Pikes Lane, Glossop, Derbyshire
Printed and bound in Great Britain

The British Bus and Truck Heritage

80 Years of Guy Motors
1914 – 1994

by

Robin Hannay

and

Stuart Fergus Broatch

Venture *publications*

CONTENTS

Introduction 5

Foreword 6

Acknowledgments 7

Frontispiece 8

1885-1914: In the beginning 9

1914-1919: The first five years 10

The Guy Cars 11

1919-1925: Peacetime production 14

1926: The six-wheelers 26

The 'thirties: Saved by the War Office 37

1939-1945: Second World War 55

1946-1958: Post-war activity 66

1958: The Commercial Motor Show 90

1961: The unthinkable happens 102

1961-1982: The final years 114

Colour selection 121

Appendices and Miscellany 129

Index 142

INTRODUCTION

The opportunity to publish this book commemorating 80 years of Guy Motors was welcomed by the Authors and Publisher – sadly the Company closed in 1982 but the memory of its products lingers on, especially in the mind of those who spent all or part of their working life at Fallings Park.

From 1914-1982 Guy Motors of Wolverhampton was one of the leaders in British automotive design. Throughout those years the company led the industry with several important innovations such as a V8 petrol engine, automatic chassis lubrication, rear-hinged doors, adjustable steering columns, 6-wheel bus and trolleybus chassis, the first bus and truck available with diesel engines, 4-wheel disc brakes, air suspension, four headlights, and many more.

The products were popular with many well-known companies in the transport industry both in the UK and overseas and Guy's customers included London Transport, Ever Ready, Lancashire United Transport & Power Co, Harrods, Edinburgh Corporation, Mobil, Northern General Transport, Milk Marketing Board, Silent Night, Red & White Services, Highland Omnibus Company, Wincanton Transport, Blue Circle Cement, Castrol, Chester Corporation, Wolverhampton Corporation, Glasso Paints, Regent Oil, and others, together with numerous smaller firms through the UK and many important overseas operators.

Sydney Guy, the founder, was a great innovator and visionary. He could be autocratic to the point of rudeness, though this was common in pre-war times when labour was easy to obtain. He took great pride in his company and its workforce and, as this book records, was instrumental in creating good industrial relations. Sadly all good things come to an end and Guy did not escape the changes in the British automobile industry during the 'sixties and 'seventies.

When production ended in 1982 the company had become part of the British Leyland empire. Leyland were keen to remove competition at a time of over capacity in the industry and closed down the famous Fallings Park Works. At the time, apart from Land Rover, Guy was the only vehicle manufacturing plant within British Leyland to make a profit, and the order book was full.

We hope that the reader will gain some feel for the company, its products, and the pride and satisfaction felt by the men and women who worked for Guy Motors.

FOREWORD

Guy Motors was an institution in Wolverhampton and the surrounding area. Even today, twelve years after production ceased at Fallings Park, ex-employees still stop for a chat when they meet up whilst out shopping or in the pub, and talk about old times.

The wages they were paid were often lower than in other local firms, but there was a feeling of being part of a team. Guy Motors was a good place to work; we had plenty of laughs but the standard of design and workmanship was second to none.

I joined Guy Motors drawing office in 1947 and soon acquired respect for the company's standing and its tradition of building solid and durable no-nonsense machinery. Although the founder, Sydney Guy, was an innovator, our customers could depend on reliable well-engineered vehicles, which often gave up to twenty years' service.

When I designed the Invincible Mark II and Warrior cabs in the late 'fifties I was inspired by Virgil Exner's designs for Chrysler, in particular the frontal aspect of the 1958 Plymouth motor car. The bumper and the grille were taken from the 1957 Ford Thunderbird; regrettably, today, vehicle design has lost much of its individuality, something we all recognised as being very important in the late 'fifties.

Many of my colleagues such as Walter Manning, Johnny Gnosil and Tony Palmer moved to the Ford Motor Company and were partially responsible for the success of the Ford marque with such excellent designs as the 'D' series and the Transit. Trevor Dudley, the chief designer who was responsible for the chassis of the Invincible and Warrior later moved to Girling. It is good to see that Guy designers can hold their own with the best.

The Jaguar era offered great promise and in Sir William Lyons the company had another individualist, and one who was not slow to recognise the value of what he had acquired at such a bargain price. The workforce responded to the opportunity and the rationalised range was a great success, proving to be a considerable money spinner.

Sadly, things moved out of Jaguar's hands and a period of decline began. Guy's very success was to prove one of the reasons why its new owner – British Leyland – wished to curtail its activities as the Lancashire-built chassis compared unfavourably in price and quality to the Fallings Park's products.

It grieved me to see the destruction of a company I had been proud to work for. The Invincibles and Warriors gave me considerable satisfaction when I saw them on the road earning their keep for operators throughout the country.

I grew up and have spent all my working life in the Wolverhampton area and look back with pride on what the people who worked at Guy and its suppliers achieved. It will not be bettered, nor, I suspect, will it ever be repeated.

Ron Thomas
Designer, Guy Motors Ltd
Wolverhampton
October 1994

Ron Thomas, left, with colleague Joe Onions, Guy's chief body designer.

ACKNOWLEDGEMENTS

The information in this book is true and complete to the best of our knowledge. The work would be much less than it is without the help, collaboration and advice of the people listed below, whose assistance is greatly acknowledged.

Annie Collet and Marie Tiséhe, Kathleen Thomas, Ron Thomas, Pauline Evans, Harry Field, Terry Greenwood, Graham Weston, John Benton, Tony Guy, Barbara Jones, Fred Berry, J. A. Stanley, R. L. Waterhouse, G. Pryce, P. Coldicott, Chris Turner, Ron Lucas, Chris Burlace, Gordon Champion, Dick Peters, Keith White, Derick Bonfield, Christopher Salman, Christine Povey, David Asplin, Tony Bacon, Brian Pickford, John Horner, Philip Dale, Jan Jensen, David Fletcher, Keith White, Lesley Ann Harnett, the late Charlie Hardy, S. Redhead, the Editor of the *Wolverhampton Star*, and members of the Guy Owner's Club. Chris Turner provided the excellent line drawings used at the end of the book.

We would also like to thank the members of the Venture Publications team: Margaret Davies, Bruce Maund, David Meredith, Carolyn Senior, John Senior, Mark Senior and Alan Townsin.

Thanks are also due to the staff at the Library of the National Motor Museum Beaulieu, The Bovington Tank Museum, Caravan World and the many people who have made Guy material available to us over the years.

The photographs have been assembled from various sources but principally from Guy official material collected by the joint authors over the considerable period of time they have been interested in the company. Many items, including all the older colour shots except the Walsall trolleybus from Photobus, came from the Senior Transport Archive in Glossop, and Roy Marshall, Geoff Atkins, Bruce Maund, Alan Townsin, and ex-employees of Guy Motors have provided black and white photographs, cuttings and the like. The modern colour material, including the cover illustration, was specially taken by John Senior. If we have inadvertently omitted any one from this list we trust they will accept our sincere apologies.

Robin Hannay
Stuart Broatch

October 1994

As the years pass, fewer Guys are seen on the roads. This former LUT Roe-bodied half-cab coach is a regular visitor to rallies in northern England.

80 years of Guy Motors -1

In the beginning – 1885-1914

For many years, Guy Motors Limited was one of Britain's best known manufacturers of commercial vehicles, buses and coach chassis. The famous North American Indian mascot was well known in over seventy countries, such was the company's success in exports.

The authors' interest in the marque stems on the one hand from rides from Hastings to Eastbourne on Southdown Guy buses in the mid 'fifties, and on the other hand from working for Guy Motors.

The authors have attempted to capture some of the flavour of Guy Motors Ltd through the products of the company, its successes and its failures.

Sydney Slater Guy was born in 1885 and as a young man lived in the King's Heath area of Birmingham. By nature he was a strong and determined character, in the words of his nephew, "a human dynamo".

Eight weeks before his seventeenth birthday Sydney Guy received a letter from the Bellis & Morcom Steam Engineering Company, dated 31st August 1901. Bellis & Morcom offered him employment and he accepted their terms, which meant being at the works in Birmingham each morning by 6.0am. Rising at 4.30am daily he took the train from King's Heath. A 53-hour week was not unusual at the time, nor were the wages of four shillings.

As was the custom in many foundries, breakfast consisted of bacon and eggs fried on shovels held over the hot coals; this was taken at 8.0am after two hours hard manual work.

Because he had shown the necessary aptitude for the work his employers were engaged in, after a few months he was offered an apprenticeship. Despite the long hours at Bellis & Morcom, Sydney Guy attended evening classes at the local Technical School in order to further his technical and engineering education.

The combination of his studies and a long working week would have severely limited Sydney Guy's social life at the time. This very arduous start in working life was shared by many other young men who would, in their later years, go on to become leaders in vehicle engineering. On finishing his apprenticeship, he joined an electrical engineering company. Here he worked with a man by the name of Harry Railing who in later years became one of the founders of the General Electric Company and who was eventually knighted for his services to industry.

A move to Humber of Coventry in 1906 as Service Manager saw Sydney Guy move from stationary steam engine manufacture to the motor industry. The Humber company had factories at Beeston, Notts and Coventry, and, until its closure in 1908, the Beeston factory produced a range of more expensive cars.

The company had been founded by Thomas Humber in 1868 for the production of bicycles. For many years the name Humber was synonymous with quality, and by 1930 the marque had evolved into an English Buick a respectable middle-class motor car.

The company also built motor cycles from 1900 to 1930 and it was one of these cycles, ridden by P. J. Evans, which won the Junior TT in 1911. With such a diverse product range, Sydney Guy's three years with Humber stood him in good stead for his later years as a manufacturer in his own right.

At that time the manager of Humber, Coventry, was Walter Phillips. His autocratic methods were typical of the period. As stated, the men were required to be at the works at 6.0am each morning, and in order to catch out any latecomers, Walter Phillips would wait outside the gates holding his pocket watch. On the stroke of six the gates were locked, to be opened again some fifteen minutes later. Any latecomers would lose one hour's pay. As they entered the work's gates, Phillips would shout, "Come on hurry now! It's you lazy buggers that live nearest the works who are always last". No workers were admitted after 6.15am and these men lost a day's pay.

It has been said that Sydney Guy was an enigma in that, on the one hand he could be ruthless when it was a question of standards, but on the other he was ahead of his time in forming a Works Council at Guy Motors in 1926 which resulted in the company being virtually strike free. This might have resulted from his own earlier experiences.

In June 1909 Sydney Guy joined the Sunbeam company of Wolverhampton. Walter Phillips said that Humber were very sorry to part with him. He was succeeded by one Roland Smith who later became Sir Roland Smith and chairman of Ford of England.

At his interview with the Sunbeam Board, after being offered and accepting the job of works manager, he was asked his age. He is reported as replying, "As you have already appointed me to the job, do you think it really matters".

At 24, Sydney Guy was works manager of a company which was soon to become one of the great vintage marques, thanks to the fertile mind of Louis Coatalen, its chief engineer, who joined the company in the same year.

The Sunbeam company derived its name from a range of japanned and tinplate products. Bicycles were produced from 1887. In 1899 the company turned to motor engineering and, from 1912, motor cycles, which were noted for their excellent finish.

Sydney Guy's salary at this time was £250 per year, with the use of a company car. His money was paid, free of any tax, in gold sovereigns. This was some four times the rate a skilled man would be paid.

Sunbeam were doing well; in the four years to 1913 profits had risen from £20,000 to approaching £200,000. As a result Sydney Guy considered that he had earned an increase in salary and a share in the profits. The directors, however, refused his request and he resigned on 30th May 1914. By now he was living comfortably in a house with adjoining farm at Finchfield, Wolverhampton. In later years the property would become an hotel.

It is likely that Sydney Guy had been planning to start up on his own for some time because production at Guy got under way very quickly. In fact the new business was registered on the very day that he left Sunbeam and the famous Fallings Park factory was in production by the September of the same year. Among prominent local backers of the enterprise was Mr Owen of Rubery Owen.

The first commercial vehicle to emerge from the new factory was a well-engineered (for the period) 30-cwt truck. Typical originality in design was evident in a number of features. The engine, a 4-cylinder side valve unit bought in from the Coventry engine manufacturer White and Poppe, was mounted on a subframe in unit with a cone clutch and a separate gear box. The assembly was suspended at three points, thus leaving the chassis frame to twist independently when the vehicle traversed uneven surfaces. The gearbox featured a direct 3rd gear with 4th geared as an overdrive. A governor, which acted only on 4th gear, limited the top speed to 30 mph. The light chassis frame was of pressed steel, again an advance on many competitors who used heavy rolled steel channel frames.

At this time buses and trucks shared the same chassis, thus the first true passenger carrying vehicle was a fourteen-seater Guy charabanc built on the 30-cwt chassis for use between Achnasheen railway station and Autbea on the coast, north of Gairloch, Scotland. Interestingly, a separate mail compartment was incorporated in the open body design.

Just as Guy Motors was starting up, the country entered the Great War. Inevitably the company became involved in the war effort and the Ministry of Munitions took over the vehicles produced, supplying them to our Russian allies. Whilst war can never be a good thing it was to benefit Guy quite clearly, and the regular flow of military contracts must have helped the new company considerably. In addition to other war work the company became the largest manufacturer in Britain of firing mechanisms for depth charges.

Two aircraft engines were also designed and manufactured. Both were radial designs, in which the crankshaft is in the centre with the cylinders placed radially round it. The first design was the 7-cylinder Wasp of 1917, followed by the more powerful 9-cylinder Dragonfly of 1918. This produced 350 bhp and was taken from the initial design to production in 24 days!

With the end of the war in 1918 there was a surplus of cheap trucks of a variety of makes for sale from the 'dump' at Slough. The ex-military vehicles were converted into trucks and buses for civilian use. They were purchased by men leaving the forces who were anxious to start up in transport, having gained experience of mechanised transport under the most difficult conditions imaginable. Many nationally known companies started at this time, and the 'twenties saw bus builders and operators proliferate.

When the war was over many companies returned to normal production. In the case of Guy Motors it was to be the beginning of peacetime production – with the 30-cwt chassis – as we shall see in the next chapter.

Above left: The original 30 cwt Guy lorry design of 1914.

Above right: 1914 Guy 'mail car' which operated over the rough tracks of the Highlands.

Left: First World War project – the seven-cylinder radial Wasp aero-engine.

80 years of Guy Motors - 3

The Guy Car Interlude

In 1915 Sydney Guy had purchased a new Type 51 Cadillac V8 and he was delighted with his new car. The type 51 had been announced in September 1914 and incorporated a 5.2-litre engine designed by D. McCall White, a Scottish-born engineer who had worked for Daimler and Napier before joining Cadillac as chief engineer.

The 70 bhp engine enabled the car to cruise effortlessly at road speeds of between 55 and 65 mph. The car was an overnight success, with Cadillac selling just over 13,000 in the 1915 model year.

As a result of his experiences with his Type 51, and the company's experience with designing and producing aero engines, plans were drawn up for a Guy V8 car.

Again, much original thought was shown in the design and layout of the V8. It was far from a copy of D. McCall White's Type 51 design. The V8 was the first Guy design to be described by the company as 'ten years ahead of its time'. The prototype was tested for 50,000 miles and part of this testing took place in North Wales where the vehicle's fuel consumption was checked over a period of thirty days.

The designer of the V8 was E. D. J. Buckney who gave a lot of thought to ease of maintenance. The V8 engine was the first to incorporate the inclined valve and detachable cylinder heads that were a feature of early Guy petrol engines. The combustion chambers were claimed to equal the efficiency of the then current overhead valve designs. The banks of cylinders were arranged at 90° and again the engine, clutch and gearbox were mounted in a subframe which was connected to the chassis by ball joints. With a cubic capacity of 4.072 litres, the 8-cylinder engine would propel the car up to speeds of 75-80 mph. However, the brakes operated via rods on the rear wheels only!

Perhaps the V8 is best remembered for its automatic chassis lubrication system, operated by a pump mounted at the front of the chassis which connected with a cam on the steering box when on full right lock.

Today it is thought that no V8 Guy cars exist. Sydney Guy's nephew, Tony Guy, has for many years tried to locate any remaining examples of the 150 produced between 1919 and 1925 but without success so far. Deliveries of the V8 commenced in the summer of 1920 and Guy Motors built the standard 4-seater tourer body. Priced at £1,474, or £1,175 in chassis form only, the Guy was in competition with some well established marques though compared with the 7.3-litre Leyland Eight for instance, which cost a staggering £3,050 when introduced at Olympia in 1920, the Guy offered good value for money.

King George V visited the Guy stand at Olympia and commented very favourably on the new model. He was

A young Sydney Guy sits proudly behind the wheel of a prototype V8 model F in 1919.

particularly taken with the beautifully machine-turned semi-polished body of the show car. Included in the price of the Guy was two year's 'free' inspection. Some chassis were bodied by specialist coach builders and indeed the works had three fine examples up to 1937, but sadly they were sold for scrap by a new works manager. How many times one hears this story of people who have no feel for the past, or anything before their time, as though nothing produced prior to their reign could possibly have any value.

The V8 had an RAC rating of 25.7 hp, and in 1921 two further additions were made to the car range. The 12 and 15.9 (RAC) hp Guy cars were priced at £660 and £750 respectively or in chassis form at £475 and £550. Their basic design followed that of the V8 chassis. In both cases the standard works body was a 4-seater tourer with hood and double screen. For export a 16.9 (RAC) hp engine was available in the larger of the two chassis. The 15.9 hp and its export version were equipped with adjustable front seats. All Guy cars had a steering column that was adjustable for height; a further refinement that was not common at the time.

At the Olympia Show of 1923 the final Guy motor car design made its appearance. This was known as the 13/36 touring chassis, available with either a 4-door saloon body or as a 4-door tourer with hood and all-weather curtains. With the 13/36 Guy introduced 4-wheel brakes. It was surprising that the 13/36 did not have an early form of hydraulic braking system knowing Sydney Guy's interest in advanced engineering. Walter Chrysler's Model B of 1924 was probably the first medium priced car with this feature.

On the new Guy 13/36 car, front hinged doors were used on the saloon body which was unusual in 1923. At

The Guy '13/36' 4-cylinder saloon of 1923. See facing page for specification.

that time the rear hinged, or 'suicide' door, as it became known as in later years, was the norm. The saloon bodied 13/36 was priced at £650 and the tourer with hood and all weather screens at £495. Production numbers were very low and it is thought that no 4-cylinder Guy cars survived.

Why did the Guy car fail? Very simply, there were too many makes and models in the market place in the early 'twenties and too few buyers. The economic climate after World War I caused problems for many firms. Some of Guy's competitors in the new car market only survived because of drastic action, the best example being Vauxhall, a very well-established and highly thought-of company. Had it not been taken over by General Motors in 1925, Vauxhall Motors would have gone by 1931.

In 1925 there was a general world slump and in later years Sydney Guy commented, "One could hardly give away a second-hand car, let alone sell a new one".

Guy V8 car in 1920 production form. Its fully automatic chassis lubrication was effected by a pump (operated from a cam on the steering mechanism) which worked every time extreme right lock was applied.

SPECIFICATION OF TOURING CAR, 13/36-H.P.

GENERAL.

The Chassis is designed and manufactured on similar lines to those of our 8-Cylinder Car, the chief deviations being that the Engine is of the 4-Cylinder type and constructed under our patented design which has been so successfully used in our various types of Commercial Motor Vehicles.

The other deviations from the 8-Cylinder Car are that the automatic Chassis Lubrication to every part has, on this less expensive Vehicle, had to be eliminated in view of the price consideration, but in almost every case, oil lubrication instead of greasers has been incorporated.

In offering this new Model, our idea has been to only incorporate in the design the principles which we have over a long period proved to be advantageous.

ENGINE DETAILS. 13/36 HAVING A BORE OF 72 M/M AND A STROKE OF 120 M/M (72 × 120).

The valves are of the mushroom type, and are placed in an inclined position. The cylinder head is detachable and water cooled, the water connections being outside the head joint, so that in the event of a leakage occurring the water cannot get into the cylinders. This patented design of cylinder head and valve arrangement is of such a construction that whilst giving all the advantages of overhead valves and detachable cylinder head, it has none of the usual disadvantages. For instance, by undoing a few nuts and without interfering with the tappets, exhaust, or inlet pipes, the head can be removed, exposing the valves and pistons for valve cleaning and grinding in or removal. The removal of the head can be made in a few minutes. The lubrication is forced by a pump into troughs for feeding the main bearings, connecting rod bearings and cam shaft and all the other moving parts. The crank and connecting rod bearings are white metal lined, and the crank is provided with a thrust bearing. Cooling by thermo-syphon and an efficient fan is provided.

IGNITION.

By a high tension magneto accessibly mounted on a cross shaft in front of the cylinders.

CARBURETTOR.

Is a "Zenith" Petrol, being suction fed by an autovac from a tank at the rear.

ELECTRIC LIGHTING AND STARTING.

DYNAMO.

Positively driven from the timing gears. The starting motor engaging with a toothed ring on the flywheel.

13/36-H.P. ENGINE UNIT. (VALVE SIDE.)

13/36 UNIT (CARBURETTOR SIDE)

CLUTCH. Leather-faced cone, particularly smooth and light in action, with easy adjustment for spring pressure.

GEAR BOX.

4 speeds and a reverse, all gears are separate and can, therefore, be replaced independently. The main shafts are carried on ball bearings, and guards are provided to prevent foreign matter getting into the races. Lubrication is by thin oil instead of the usual and unsatisfactory oil and grease mixture. The change speed is attached directly to the gear box, so that the jamming of the mechanism, due to the want of alignment and distortion, is impossible. The levers are on the right hand side. The gears and shafts are in special nickel alloy steel.

BRAKES.

Foot brake operates on all 4 wheels, of the internal expanding type. Hand brake operates in rear hubs with shoes, independent of the foot brake shoes.

SPRINGS.

All are of the semi-elliptic type, the rear springs being underslung. The springs shackles are lubricated by oil. Shock absorbers fitted to all springs.

BACK AXLE.

This is of the semi-floating type. The drive is by spiral bevels, and these, together with the differential complete, are carried in a bevel housing which is separate from the axle case, and by removing the hubs and withdrawing the axle shafts the whole of the gears and differential can be removed in one unit. Lubrication is by oil, which is automatically fed to all gears, differential and road wheels.

FRONT AXLE.

Is of "H" Section, specially designed to withstand the additional stresses of front wheel brakes. The swivel pins have renewable bushes and the wear on the heads is taken on thrust bearings. The lubrication of the swivel pins is by oil

STEERING.

Is of the worm and wheel type. The steering column, which can be raised or lowered at different angles to suit different drivers, is steadied by a universal bracket from the dashboard, and can be lowered on to the chassis if desired for shipment. A complete worm wheel is used and the lever arranged to fit in four places, if necessary, thus giving much longer life of wheel.

FOUR-DOOR SALOON, SHOWING ACCESSIBILITY OF SEATS WITHOUT DISTURBING PASSENGERS.

Price £650 complete

STEERING CONNECTIONS.

The side steering and front steering rods are tubular and fitted with our patent oil lubricated ball joints.

RADIATOR. Film Type.

WHEELS AND TYRES.

Five detachable artillery steel wheels are supplied, fitted with 30 × 3½ Dunlop cord tyres. Disc wheels can be supplied at an extra charge.

FRAME. Pressed steel.

INSTRUMENT BOARD.

Carries Electric Light switches, clock, ammeter, oil gauge, dashboard lamp, dimmer switch for head lamps, and speedometer.

SPEEDOMETER. Is gear driven from the gear box.

LUGGAGE CARRIER, NUMBER PLATES.

13/36-H.P. Chassis Dimensions.

ENGINE. R.A.C. Rating. 12.8. Bore and Stroke. 72 m/m × 120 m/m. 4-Cylinder.

GROUND CLEARANCE. 9".

TRACK. 4' 4". TYRES. 30 × 3½ Dunlops, with one spare.

WHEELBASE. 9' 4½".

Peacetime Production 1919-1925

1919 saw peacetime production begin, and the arrival of the Guy charabanc which utilised the 30-cwt chassis. Bus bodies were also fitted to the 30-cwt chassis, creating fore runners of the modern minibus. With solid tyres and hard seating, comfort for passengers was somewhat lacking. However, these small Guy vehicles were well thought of at the time.

With a view to improving passenger comfort experiments took place in 1920 with the Holden pneumatic suspension system. This consisted of two channels attached to the chassis and body members, with a pneumatic tube between them. However, because of rapid advances in tyre technology at the time which resulted in the introduction of the pneumatic tyres for both buses and trucks, the idea was abandoned.

In the same year a new 2½-ton chassis was introduced at the first post-war commercial motor show.

Another introduction in 1920 was a truck fitted with SPUD wheels, as fitted to agricultural tractors of the period. The vehicle was designed to appeal to farmers who required a light truck that was capable of being driven over all types of terrain without losing its grip. The wheels were made of steel with wide angled flanges which thus lowered the pressure on the ground and gave a good grip.

In 1921 the governor was omitted from the specification of the 30-cwt chassis. This device was never popular with drivers who appreciated the overdrive top gear that reduced engine speeds and improved the fuel economy but disliked having their maximum speed restricted to 30 mph, even though the law only allowed them to travel at 12mph!

At the Royal Agricultural Show held in Sydney, Australia in 1922, 2½- and 3-ton chassis were exhibited. They caused a lot of interest amongst potential purchasers, in particular from bus operators. Guy Motors benefited from some good orders as a result of attending this show.

Engines in this period were all 4-cylinder designs, ranging in size from 2.72 litres to 4½ litres.

The company's new 2½-ton chassis were already attracting well established names such as Peek Frean's Biscuits and Weston's Cider and Perry.

The year 1923 saw the arrival of an unusual twin-engined road/rail vehicle. It was designed to meet the requirements of South African Railways. In all some 25 were built. Designed by the railway's Chief Engineer for use where there was a need for a vehicle which could operate on either railway tracks or road and be capable of shunting freight wagons at railway marshalling yards, the

A truck fitted with SPUD wheels. Introduced in 1920, it was claimed to be first truck designed for farmers.

A Guy charabanc of 1919 seen at the top of Lynmouth Hill, the well-known 1 in 4½ Devon gradient. Features of the vehicle included: 4-cylinder engine with inclined valves, three-point suspension, transmission type foot brake, four-speed-plus-reverse gearbox, double reduction rear axle, pressed steel frame, cone clutch, and carbide lamps. The distinctive Guy logo can be seen cast into the radiator shell.

The patented tipping body on this 2½ tonner was advertised as being able to carry two 25 cwt loads and tip them independently. Built by Jennings of Sandbach it was so designed that when the body was released at the front, it could be wound up by the driver to discharge the load.

Above: Guy truck production in the 'twenties, shown in a publicity photograph taken around 1928. Types ranging from the JA 15-cwt model up to the BA, B and BB range with left-hand steering for export can be seen. The chassis nearest the camera is a 1 ton model (see page 23, upper photograph). This is followed by what appears to be a Model D bus chassis. The second half of the decade was a good period for the company, thanks to a buoyant market and the company's reputation for innovative design.

Left: This 1923 photograph, showing the unique road-rail vehicle under construction, gives some idea of the size of the main assembly hall at the time. The early 'twenties saw many men sacked due to the economic climate after the Great War. The construction of the Fallings Park Works in 1914 was a remarkable achievement for a young man of 29 years of age.

Foot: All Guy vehicles were tested for 30 miles on the public highway before being despatched. Thirty miles in the road-rail vehicles seen here would have been an uncomfortable experience ! The photograph shows the detachable front bogie on the leading vehicle. The crude steering layout was similar to that found on a horse drawn cart or traction engine where the complete axle is designed to turn in relation to the chassis in order to negotiate sharp corners.

A Guy 30 cwt tractor unit with trailer for hauling timber – owned by John Eade & Sons of Brighton.

design was successful except for the problem of negotiating points. The engine's torque was transmitted via a prop shaft which drove two large wheels at the rear which ran outside the railway track sleepers. At the front there was a detachable bogie which was removed for road use.

Some 24 years earlier, Thornycrofts of Basingstoke produced one of the world's first articulated commercial vehicles which won the Premier Award at the Liverpool Self-Propelled Traffic Association's Trial of 1898. In the early 'twenties the articulated commercial vehicle was not a common sight as it is today. Because of the intense competition at the time, it would appear that Sydney Guy was looking at new designs, trying to anticipate future needs. With this in mind, in addition to the road-rail vehicle, he also introduced an articulated 6-wheel commercial vehicle and a 2½-3-ton battery-electric vehicle for refuse collection.

Electric vehicles were quite successful, particularly in the United States of America during the first 25 years of the 20th century. Some well-known companies put designs into production, ranging from cars to commercial vehicles. Early pioneers included John M. Studebaker, who was known throughout his life as 'Wheelbarrow Johnny'. He was quoted as saying of petrol engine vehicles that they were "clumsy, dangerous, noisy brutes [which] stink to high heaven, break down at the worst possible moment and are a public nuisance."

The Studebaker brothers sold the Studebaker Electric from 1902-1910. With a range of 40 miles on a single charging, it would trundle along at 15 mph. Such cars were popular with lady drivers.

The most successful battery electric products were commercial vehicles and the most successful manufacturer was the Walker Vehicle Company of Chicago, Illinois, which was in business from 1906-1942. One of its former customers, Harrods Ltd of London has a restored 1919 Model K van which was a great favourite of the late John Betjeman and is often shown at old vehicle events.

In 1923 Bournemouth Corporation bought three chassis from Guy Motors, which were then fitted with 16-seater toastrack bodies by local coachbuilder J. & A. Steane. They proved very reliable on Route 15 between Bournemouth Pier and Boscombe Pier.

A 1923 Guy Promenade Runabout based on a special version of the J chassis. They were popular with seaside resorts, with Bournemouth and Portsmouth running examples. Producing models with small wheels, giving a low load line where speeds would be low, was one of Guy's specialities.

In 1923 an agreement between John Morris in Manchester and Guy Motors resulted in the latter supplying J-type chassis as the basis of a fire engine. This vehicle was exhibited at the 1924 Motor Show in Wembley and was used as a demonstrator for two years before being sold to Cheddleton Paper Mills in Staffordshire. When withdrawn in 1967 it went for preservation.

Below: In 1924 Guys supplied their first vehicles to the War Department. The majority went to the Army but several were used by the Royal Navy. The one in front is a 2½ tonner and following it is a 30 cwt model.

These small Guys were known as the Promenade Runabouts and they were popular with other seaside resorts. The following year a further three Runabouts were ordered by Bournemouth.

Wadhams, the coachbuilders from Waterlooville, further east along the coast, built five 15-seat bodies on Guy J-type chassis for Portsmouth Corporation, for use between Clarence Pier and South Parade Pier.

A patent emergency exit at the rear was an advanced feature of a small one-man-operated bus shown in 1923. This was typical of the company's advanced thinking and it would be several years before it was a legal requirement.

Guy Motors supplied the Army with some General Service vehicles, fitted with pneumatic tyres, in the same year. This was followed a year later by an order from the Crown Agents, Admiralty and War Office for half-track versions. The rear tracks gave the vehicles excellent grip but mud and grit caused premature wear in the track joints.

A chassis designed specifically for bus use was introduced in 1924. It was one of the first British dropped frame chassis. Available in three wheel bases of 13ft 4in, 15ft 3in and 16ft 5in and retaining the designations also used on corresponding straight-framed models BA, B and BB respectively, the new designs met with approval from bus operators. The largest model, the BB could seat up to 30 passengers. The lower centre of gravity made life easier for drivers, with improved handling, and the reduced number of steps for boarding the vehicle would have been

18/20. SEATER BUS. (GUY CHASSIS)
BODY BUILT BY CHAS. H. ROE (1923) LTD.

appreciated by passengers. Power came from a 4-cylinder engine of 4½-litres capacity, which was connected to a 4-speed gear box, with final drive by worm axle. Early orders for the new design included several which specified Guy bodywork.

Burton-on-Trent Corporation, who over the years would prove to be the company's most loyal customer in the passenger service vehicle market, purchased two model BA buses fitted with Guy 20-seat front-entrance bodies. They were followed by an additional order for five model B buses with seating capacities varying from 20 to 25.

Model BB buyers included Keighley, Leicester, Walsall, West Bromwich, Birkenhead, National Omnibus & Transport and Burton-on-Trent, whose last two vehicles were eventually fitted with Gardner 4LW engines. A 6-cylinder engine was available from 1925, fitted in a BB frame. The model designation changed to BK or Premier Six. The new engine was a Daimler-Knight sleeve valve unit of 5.76 litres. This engine was used in the Daimler 35 hp

(RAC) car, the ADC 802 double-decker and, later, the Daimler CF6.

The straight-framed BA, B and BB continued, now purely as goods models, the basic design being derived from the immediate post-war 2½-ton model, which had been designated type B from the beginning, though this was not used for publicity material at that period, the standard wheelbase then being 12ft 4½. The 2-ton BA had been addedd in 1921, with 10ft 4in wheelbase, and the 3-ton BB in 1923, at 14ft 4½, though, for 1925, the BA became 12ft 4½in and the B 13ft 4½in. All still had solid tyres as standard at that date, and the Guy 4½-litre 4-cylinder engine retained the 4in bore and 5½in stroke as used for this series since 1919.

Guy Motors was able to produce a very wide variety of bodies to the requirements of its customers. The last five years of what has become known as the jazz age, were ones in which Guy Motors would show the bus industry the quality of its innovative design.

Above: Vintage caravan comfort ! This handsome motor caravan was built in 1924 for a Mr Dennis of Pendine on a Guy 2-ton chassis. It provided a combined lounge, dining and sleeping saloon, with a verandah at the rear of the vehicle. Ample cupboard and locker accommodation was provided.

Right: A large number of J type vans were bought by W. Whiteley, a well-known store in London, in 1924. Pneumatic tyres were now standard on this model which was designed for a 25 cwt payload. Another London store using Guy vans was John Barkers who chose the 30 cwt 'O' model on pneumatic tyres. This had larger tyres and a longer wheelbase than the 'J'. Like most vehicles in this era, windscreens were fitted but side windows were not – in case the driver became too warm and fell asleep !

Below: Many famous names appeared on Guy vehicles. Amongst them was Harrods who placed several repeat orders including this 3 ton BB delivered in 1925. It had the optional pneumatic tyres which were becoming available in larger sizes.

Above: Two-tonner low-loader fitted with a Lonsdale reversible horse box built by Dennis Bros. & Son Ltd of Kensington. The main feature of this vehicle was that it allowed horses to walk in and out without a steep ramp. As the legal limit was 12 mph at the time the small wheels may not have been too much of a disadvantage on a long journey. Refuse collection bodies also were fitted to this type of chassis, making it easier to empty the dustbins into a lower level body.

Below: A model BB 3 ton fixed-sided truck on solid tyres for carrying milk. It was bought by the Retail Dairymans Mutual Limited, London W2. This is an early example of bodywork for crate and churn movement of milk. The body is slung low over the chassis. Flooring was slatted wood with gaps to allow for bottle breakage; the chains were detachable for side loading. On many of these vehicles the steel brackets were made and supplied by Pinks Forging Ltd of Sheffield. Rope hooks are fitted to the undersides of the body for roping down the load.

GUY VEHICLES for MUNICIPAL WORK.

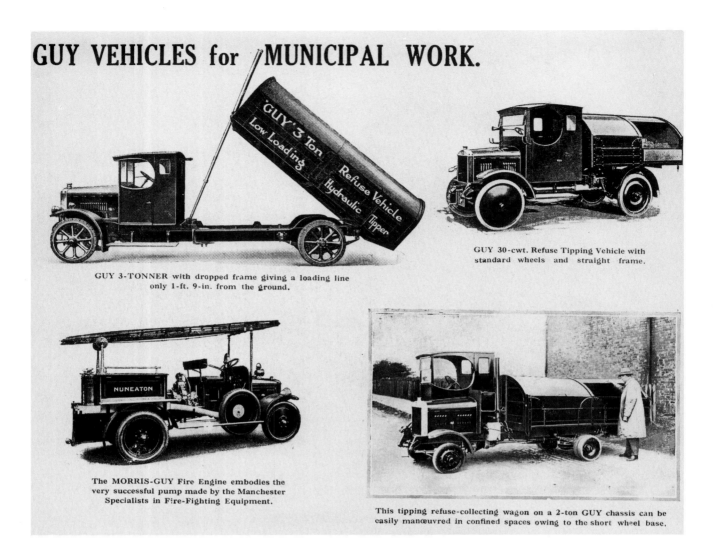

GUY 3-TONNER with dropped frame giving a loading line only 1-ft. 9-in. from the ground.

GUY 30-cwt. Refuse Tipping Vehicle with standard wheels and straight frame.

The MORRIS-GUY Fire Engine embodies the very successful pump made by the Manchester Specialists in Fire-Fighting Equipment.

This tipping refuse-collecting wagon on a 2-ton GUY chassis can be easily manœuvred in confined spaces owing to the short wheel base.

Municipal vehicles represented an important side of Guy's business, and in 1925 they produced a modified chassis with a stepped frame for bus work . It was adapted for use as a refuse collector, enabling a lower loading height to be achieved.

In 1925 the 15 cwt 'grew up' to a 1-tonner and was advertised as the lowest-priced all-British vehicle of this capacity, as distinct from 'touring car conversions'. This example was supplied to Chesham and Wycombe Cooperative Society, with an 11ft-long van body.

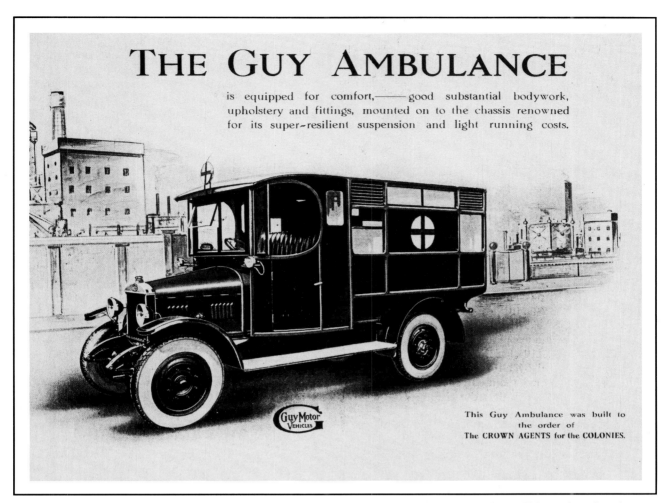

THE GUY AMBULANCE

is equipped for comfort,——good substantial bodywork, upholstery and fittings, mounted on to the chassis renowned for its super-resilient suspension and light running costs.

This Guy Ambulance was built to the order of The CROWN AGENTS for the COLONIES.

Guys had a well-equipped bodyshop and one of their products in the mid-1920s was a complete ambulance. This was based on the 1 ton JA chassis, but had different springs, plus shock absorbers on both axles to improve the ride. Two stretcher cases and four sitting patients could be accommodated in the standard body, but other options were available.

The low-loading versions of the B-series chassis introduced a significantly different look to Guy's passenger range, as conveyed by this B model dating from 1928 – note the floor level, noticeably lower than the frame level at the front of the chassis, and with body waistline lower than the bonnet top. It was one of three supplied to Burton-on-Trent Corporation, which had chosen Guy BA and B vehicles for its first order for buses in 1924, and was to continue to standardise on Guy chassis until 1961 - the company's most loyal customer for passenger models. The 25-seat bodywork was also by Guy, and this example has the radiused top corners to the side windows, an unusual feature at that date and characteristic of Guy bodywork of the period. Other noteworthy features include the radiator, with slightly rounded shape by that date and with the Red Indian 'feathers in our cap' mascot, to be found on many later Guy models, on the filler. The oval bodybuilder's transfer, using the large G, as in the advertisement above, can be seen behind the front mudguard.

Important events occurred in 1926 as far as Guy Motors was concerned. Of these, the General Strike was the one in which the company was affected very little but which would leave its mark in the changed working conditions in Britain for many men and women in the post World War II years.

Much has been written about 'The Land fit for Heroes' to which soldiers returned with heightened expectations after 1918. For many, their living and working conditions were appalling but there were some notable exceptions among the employers of the time. Two companies that stand out are Guy and Vauxhall. Both practised better industrial relations for their time than the majority of their competitors. Interestingly, both formed committees where management and workers together could endeavour to sort out problems.

Sydney Guy led the way, setting up a Works Committee after the General Strike of 1926 which offered proportional representation and which proved effective in preventing strikes. In fact, apart from a few employees who walked out in the General strike, the company was virtually strike free.

Over the years Sydney Guy was very fortunate in having round him some outstanding people. One such person was Frank Mansel, who in later years became Mayor of Wolverhampton and Chairman of the Wolverhampton Transport Committee. Frank Mansel joined Guy Motors in 1926. He was a strong trade unionist and was always anxious to promote goodwill. It is likely that he was a major influence in the setting up of the Works Committee.

After 1926 all Guy employees had to sign the following declaration:

'Are you a member of a Trade Union?
What Union (if any)?

"I agree, if engaged, to observe all the rules and regulations of Guy Motors Limited and particularly those special rules relating to the avoidance of disputes, as follows:

"I agree not under any circumstances, to cease work or go slow until the matter under dispute has been reported in writing within 48 hours notice by the Works Committee to the General Works Manager who the firm undertake will reply within 48 hours. Failing a satisfactory reply, the matter, in writing, shall be referred to the Managing Director within 48 hours notice, who undertakes to reply within 48 hours. If the reply is unsatisfactory, the committee can refer the matter to the Executive of the Trades Union, who will communicate with the Managing Director and, providing the answer received is not satisfactory, then, and not till then, will I down tools."

Sydney Guy's son Robin has described the takeover of the failing Star Engineering Co Ltd of Wolverhampton which took place in 1926 as "ill judged". However, it needs to be looked at with the facts that were at hand in 1926.

The Wall Street crash was three years away and it is likely that Sydney Guy thought of making another attempt at the motor car market. Like many small manufacturers, Star had a very extensive range of motor cars by the mid 'twenties. Seven-bearing crankshafts were a feature of the company's later 6-cylinder designs. By 1929 these were being sold as the 18 hp (RAC) and Comet and 21 hp (RAC) Planet. After the takeover they received handsome new bodies and were very fully equipped with a one-shot chassis lubrication system, thermostatically controlled radiator shutters and a built-in jacking system. The events that started with the Wall Street crash of 24th October 1929 would make such motor cars no longer viable.

The most famous Star was the Flyer, which was developed from a 20-seat low-loading bus chassis introduced in 1927. The original 4-cylinder engine was replaced by a 6-cylinder 3.2-litre unit in an attempt to move into the light coach market, where vehicles such as the Reo Speedwagon were very popular on account of high performance and reasonable initial price. The Flyer's 6-cylinder engine was later replaced by a larger 3.6-litre unit, together with vacuum brakes.

As a result of the company's progressive bus design, Guy Motors received a massive order for 170 Premier Six vehicles powered by Daimler Knight sleeve valve engines when a representative of the Rio de Janeiro Tramway and Power Company called unannounced at the works one day, liked what he saw and immediately placed the order. In May 1936 Leyland's technical director, Dr H. F. Haworth, visited Rio de Janeiro during the course of a business tour of South America and commented in his report, "normally one would have expected these (Guys) to be on the scrap heap by now, and I was very surprised on seeing them in such excellent condition on the streets of Rio. . . I do not see any reason why they should not last for ever, and, as they are the only large machines running in Rio, they do not get outdated by fashion. I rode on some of them, and apart from slightly noisy gears, they ran very well". Praise indeed from a competitor who concluded that there was not much future for Leyland in Rio !

The J-type was replaced in 1926 by the 'ON'. It was completely redesigned, having a new 4-cylinder 3.3-litre engine. Pneumatic tyres were standard, as was a 12-volt electrical system. Intended for a 30 cwt payload, this tipper was bought by Leicester Tramways and Motor Omnibus Department. The chassis cost £348 with a further £25 if front wheel brakes were required.

Above: The Star Engineering Co Ltd of Wolverhampton was taken over in 1926. This Star Flyer bus chassis of a few years later is shown outside Guy Motor's Johannesburg premises. In its day the Flyer was renowned for its lively performance.

Below: A well-known chemist added this JA 1-tonner to its fleet in 1926; the rack on the roof was for carrying empty tins. The specification included pneumatic tyres on the front axle, and a bulb-horn.

Following the introduction of the dropped-frame version of the B series chassis in 1924, Guy announced a forward-control version of the BB, designated FBB, in 1926. This produced a vehicle which competed in the growing market for drop-frame buses seating 30-35 passengers, and generally with 4-cylinder engines in which its contemporaries included the ADC 416, Bristol B, Dennis E, Leyland Lion PLSC and Maudslay ML3. The Great Western Railway placed 55 in service in 1927, probably the largest fleet of the type in Britain.

The chassis design of the FBB was largely as used in the Premier Six, though the standard engine was still the 4.5litre side valve Guy unit, much as used in the standard BB. The wheelbase was 16ft 5in, a choice of underslung worm or double reduction axle was offered; 4-wheel brakes were still not regarded as essential and were thus an extra cost option.

A lightweight chassis suitable for carrying 16-20 passengers was announced in the same year. The new chassis weighed 26 cwt and was Guy's first example of unit construction whereby the engine (in this case a new Guy OHV 4-cylinder 19.2 hp (RAC) unit) was bolted to the clutch bellhousing and gearbox. The clutch was still of the cone type. Easy access was provided to allow the leather part of the clutch to be dressed when necessary. An underslung worm axle of the horizontal banjo type, with a removable upper cover, took the final drive to the rear wheels.

A 4-cylinder OHV engine and unit construction for the engine, clutch and gearbox were features of the lightweight model 'ON' chassis which was introduced in 1926.

During the first half of 1926 Guy Motors introduced the BX model. The BX was Britain's first low frame 6-wheel double-deck chassis. Designed to accommodate up to 62 passengers seated, the CX was in 1926 an advanced design. An unusual feature for a British double-deck design was the normal control layout which would have been familiar to anyone who had visited New York.

The company supplied the British Army in the same year with a rigid 6-wheel truck in which both rear axles were powered and the bogie would fully articulate. Known as the BAX model, it was purchased by the War Office.

In 1928 the FBAX was introduced, which was simply a Forward Control version of the original. The greater part of the War Office order was for the later version or FBAX which stayed in production until 1940.

A 6-wheel model BAX Guy under test in 1926. Both rear axles were driven. The forward-control FBAX introduced two years later stayed in production until 1940. Are the men in the bowler hats from the War Office ? The knowledge gained in designing the BAX/FBAX range was used to good effect with the 6-wheel model CX bus chassis.

Right: Interest from haulage operators in 3-axle chassis was centred more on the possibilities for additional payload, Other benefits claimed were better braking, reduced wheelspin and skidding. The latter were related to the absence of a third differential between the bogie axles, but this imposed severe stresses on propellor shafts, leading to failures.

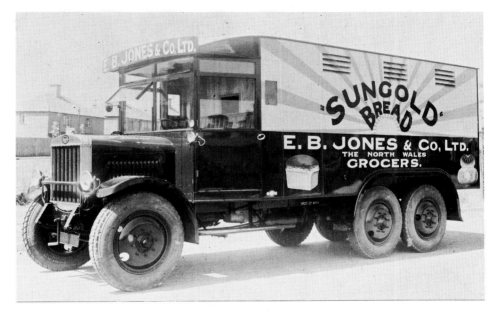

Wolverhampton Corporation 47 (DA 9047), placed in service in July 1926, was a historic vehicle, Britain's first 6-wheel double-deck motor bus, though Karrier had shown a prototype 6-wheel bus chassis at the 1925 Show. Guy announced its initial range of 6-wheel bus chassis for general sale the same month as the Wolverhampton prototype appeared. It was of type BX as built, with a slightly enlarged version of Guy's 4-cylinder sidevalve engine, of 5.1-litre capacity and developing 60bhp. The body was by Dodson. The choice of normal-control layout for a large double-decker had become fairly unusual by that date in Britain, and could have been influenced by practice in the United States, where it remained standard for front-engined models much longer. This Wolverhampton vehicle and some others of the type are believed to have been rebuilt to later specification and reclassified CX, the latter not being introduced until 1927.

Birmingham Corporation's first venture with 6-wheel buses was the placing in service of its 208 (OP 237) into service in the latter part of 1926. This was a Guy BKX model, the 'K' signifying the use of a Knight-type 6-cylinder sleeve valve engine, actually the 5.7-litre unit of 35hp RAC rating made by Daimler. It had a Short Bros body seating 58, the profile in this case not only suiting the normal-control chassis but with the front of the upper deck set back by about 1ft behind the windscreen – the idea of extending the upper-deck forward over the cab was often to be approached with great caution for several more years. The floor line was comparatively low, even though a misleading impression is given by the way the skirt panels were not extended much below this level, as also evident in the vehicle shown below. It seems that it may not have proved very satisfactory, since Birmingham records show that a 'new chassis' was supplied by Guy Motors in 1927 – it was withdrawn in 1933, many of these early 6-wheel buses having quite short lives.

Below: Oldham Corporation took three Guy six-wheel double-deckers with 54-seat bodywork by Roe in late 1926. There seems to be some doubt as to the type, both CX and FCX having been quoted, though again, these names had not been introduced when they were built. It seems clear from the typically B-series style of radiator seen in these bodybuilder's photographs that, as originally supplied, they were of BX or possibly BKX type. It is significant that a Daimler engine is reported to have been fitted to one in 1928, rather suggesting that, here again, some change of specification may have occurred. The overall appearance was soon to look curiously old-fashioned, though the use of open stairs gave a more balanced look with the normal-control layout. At that time, it was usual for the rear platform of double-deckers to be at the same height as the saloon floor, requiring two steps up from ground level to reach it.

A prototype BX was tested by Wolverhampton Corporation, entering service in July 1926. A Dodson body was fitted. This featured an open rear staircase as usual at that date.

A Guy 5.1-litre 4-cylinder engine powered the vehicle which was fitted into the usual Guy subframe. A similar chassis was fitted with a 58-seat Short Bros. body and tried out by Birmingham Corporation.

Whilst Guy had been busy with its petrol-engined vehicles it had not ignored the developments in electric propulsion which were becoming a potential threat to its business. In its native town, Wolverhampton, the Corporation's transport department was rapidly becoming one of the leaders in the use of the trolleybus – a vehicle which was rapidly gaining in popularity.

In 1923-26 Wolverhampton had bought its first trolley buses – 32 Dodson bodied single-deckers – based on the Tilling-Stevens TS6 forward control petrol-electric bus chassis.

Not long after the arrival of the new trolleybuses, a Mr C. Owen Silvers took over as general manager of the Corporation Transport Department. Owen Silvers could see that with better accommodation the trolleybus was an ideal vehicle in urban areas.

The Corporation had shown that the trolleybus was cheaper to operate than the petrol-engined motor bus of this time. Running costs per mile in 1926 were calculated by Wolverhampton to be 12.26d for the motor bus compared with 11.46d for the trolleybus.

The other reason for interest in the trolleybus was the cost of replacing worn out tram systems. For example, in December 1924 Darlington Corporation claimed that to relay existing tracks and purchase new cars would cost

A production example of the BAX military six-wheeler. Army lorries retained the open cab, without windscreen and no protection other than a folding hood, much as used in the 1914-18 war, long after civilian lorries had enclosed cabs.

£160,000. However, it was stated, that for £35,000 all existing tram routes could be converted to trolleybus operation – quite a saving if the figures were correct!

Later in 1926 a revolutionary trolleybus chassis was introduced, the BTX. Overnight it made all other trolleybus designs obsolete. Based on the recently introduced 6-wheel double-deck bus chassis, the new design would enable local authorities to change over to what was claimed to be a cheaper mode of transport and take up their tram tracks.

The first BTX trolleybus, which in 1926 became number 33 in the fleet of Wolverhampton Corporation, seen undergoing a tilt test. The somewhat intrepid passengers are Guy employees – bags of sand were generally used to simulate the appropriate loading without the associated risk – however small – of an accidental tip over. However, a restraining cable can be seen running out over the open stair handrail of the Dodson body. Number 33 was returned to Guy Motors eleven years later at a time when it was hoped to start a company museum – alas this did not occur and it was scrapped in 1941.

Above: Wolverhampton Corporation also placed the first 6-wheeled trolleybus in service in 1926. This was one of the following year's delivery of fifteen, carrying a Dodson 61-seat body, by this time with enclosed stairs. A similar vehicle was at the 1927 Show.

Below: A Guy 6-wheel chassis showing the front-mounted motor and twin differentials on the rear bogie. Guy retained the front-mounted motor on its trolleybuses right up to 1939 – it allowed a larger diameter unit to be used and this permitted finer 'notching' of the power supply, with smoother acceleration than on other trolleybuses.

There were four models in the initial trolleybus range. Model BT32 was designed as a single-deck two-axle vehicle, with seating for 35 passengers, with a double-deck version designated BT48. The others were three-axle designs. They were the BTX60 and BTX66 which could accommodate 60 and 66 passengers respectively. The BTX66 was one foot longer and designed for double or single-deck bodywork.

The first BT chassis were fitted with Rees Stevens electrical equipment. Later this was changed to equipment manufactured by The Electric Construction Co Ltd of Bushbury.

Regenerative braking was a very advanced feature of the Guy trolleybus chassis. With this system electrical power was fed back into the overhead line from the motor when the power pedal was released. Seven years would elapse before any of the competition caught up with this feature. The Wolverhampton Corporation trolleybuses were a success and, no doubt, Owen Silvers was a happy man.

A small capacity bus chassis built for 16-seater bodywork, the OND was also introduced this year. Local Midlands operator Walsall Corporation bought an 18-seat OND in 1926.

Guy BTX Rees Roturbo demonstrator in Nottingham livery as its fleet number 25 and photographed in King Street, Nottingham in October 1930 outside the Prudential Assurance Offices. Period dress of cloche hat and fur coat are in evidence on the approaching pedestrian. This body style, typical of Guy double-deck bodywork of the period, with wide corner panels at the front of the upper-deck 'piano-front', is very similar to those built for Johannesburg in 1930.

Cape Town's first trolleybus, a Guy BTX, was delivered in 1930. The vehicle is shown here near the foot of Table Mountain.

A model BT32 single-deck trolleybus built for operation in Japan. Guy's trolleybus designations – clearly this was simply 'B Trolleybus 32-seat' – continued unchanged into the 'thirties even though the detail design altered to correspond with the C and then D series motor buses. This example is thought to date from the early 'thirties.

The following year, 1927, saw Guy Motors widen the range of model BX bus chassis. There was now a choice of three wheelbase lengths, ranging from 16ft 7in to 19ft 1½in. The largest chassis was also advertised as being suitable for single-deck or double-deck bodies with seating for up to 74 people. In addition to a forward-control model, the FBKX was introduced, powered by a 5.76-litre 6-cylinder Daimler Knight sleeve valve engine. This more powerful engine was also available in the original normal control chassis which was then known as the BKX. The 4-cylinder engine was now available in the FBX forward-control chassis.

Guy buses had first made their appearance on the streets of London a year earlier in 1926 when Mason Brothers of New Southgate, the proprietors of Uneedus services, bought two examples fitted with single-deck bodies by Strachan & Brown. It took many months of discussion before Scotland Yard, which was responsible for the licensing of buses in London, would allow the double-deck 6-wheelers on the streets of the capital. In all, some thirteen London independent operators bought the new Guy double-deckers.

An advanced gas producer truck was one of Guy Motors new offerings for 1927. The vehicle was designed for operation in the more remote parts of the world where the supply of petrol was not always reliable. The Australian Government, amongst others, placed orders. The recommended fuel was charcoal and a saving of 94 per cent was claimed in fuel costs.

One municipal authority is said to have run its vehicles on sewer gas. However, the best example of the producer gas vehicles' adaptability was demonstrated when Guy Motors had an enquiry as to whether the design would burn camel dung. A local farmer was able to supply some cow dung, which after drying was found to be very suitable and a reasonable order was obtained.

Facing page

The famous motto 'Feathers in our cap' was already in use as an advertising slogan in the 'twenties, as seen here, though it was to become more familiar in later years adorning the head-dress of the Red Indian radiator filler mascot. Six-wheelers have the top positions in this montage of the company's products.

Below: Two illustrations of the gas producer vehicle of 1927. It was claimed that it would run on 'almost anything combustible'.

There was intense rivalry to get the first 6-wheel doubledecker on to the streets of London. The newly-formed London Public Omnibus Co, an independent concern, bought several Guy 6wheelers in 1927, and for many years Guy Motors publicity used this photograph of what it claimed was the first 6-wheel doubledecker to be licensed in the capital. The story went that the London General Omnibus Co had put an ADC, actually LS1, the first of the 802-model, in service 'just before the Guy, but due to lack of electric lighting, it had to be withdrawn at dusk each day until completed'. In fact, LS1 entered service on route 16A, Cricklewood to Victoria Station, on 4th June, 1927 from Cricklewood garage. The first of the London Public fleet, its GS1, did not enter service until 9th September, on route 529 from Winchmore Hill to Victoria Station. It seems a little strange if it really took the mighty LGOC three months to sort out whatever lighting problems there might have been on LS1, and in any case by 20th August, LS2 had already joined it on the 16A. Even so, Guy's achievement in developing the 6-wheel bus and trolleybus in Britain cannot be belittled.

Leeds placed four FCX models in service in the summer of 1928. These vehicles had a very short life and all had been withdrawn by 1932, though the chassis of two of the batch were sold to Derby Corporation. Roe built the 38-seat bodywork.

Leyland Motors borrowed two vehicles from Blackpool Corporation in 1927 and compared them with the newly-completed Leyland Titan TD1. The contrast was dramatic, to say the least! Here Blackpool's FCX is tilted in Leyland's South Works as part of the comparison – the nearside wheel has been apparently turned to help secure the chassis, though this would defeat the object of the normal tilt test.

The company's range of passenger vehicle chassis was further enlarged with the arrival of the Model C range in 1927. A new Guy side valve 6-cylinder engine replaced the Daimler Knight unit.

The new range was available in the following variations:

Model	Control	Wheels	Wheelbase	Seats
C	Normal	4	16ft 5in	28
FC	Forward	4	16ft 5in	32
CX	Normal	6	16ft 7in	32
CX	Normal	6	18ft 6in	66
CX	Normal	6	19ft 1½in	39
CX	Normal	6	19ft 1½in	72
FCX	Forward	6	same variations as for CX.	

It was around this time that forward-control was proving more popular for buses as more passengers could be accommodated on a given wheelbase though coaches used for touring often retained the normal control layout. As a result of this trend the normal-control CX range was taken out of production almost immediately.

In 1929 a new overhead valve engine was fitted to the new OND model. The chassis was designed for a 20-seat body. Later a forward-control version was put into production. This was followed in 1932 by the Victory model which offered increased performance through using a 55 bhp 3.6-litre 6-cylinder engine. The forward-control version of the OND was known as the ONDF. Wolverhampton Corporation and West Bromwich Corporation opted for vehicles from this range.

The 1920s was a period of change. In the world of motor engineering, pneumatic tyres, chromium plating, cellulose paint, improved casting techniques and pressings were some of the advances made by motor vehicle manufacturers during this decade.

For the first 30 years of the 20th century Dennis Bros. of Guildford, Surrey were leading producers of all types of commercial vehicles and buses. In 1927 Dennis Bros. reported a profit of £335,000 and made a bid to acquire Guy Motors which almost succeeded. The following year their profits increased to £361,000 and a merger with Leyland Motors was contemplated. However, over-generous dividend payments to shareholders, even in the early 'thirties, meant that Dennis Bros. became less of a threat in terms of sales, due to lack of investment. From 1925 the profits produced by Guy Motors rapidly improved. By 1929 the company had reached a peak.

However, the Wall Street crash of October saw £1 shares written down to ten shillings. Further reduction occurred, resulting in a 95 per cent loss of capital when shares fell to one shilling. As a direct result of the Wall Street crash Guy Motors nearly went under. Sydney Guy must have bitterly regretted taking over Star.

In 1927 Express Motors Ltd of Darlington had introduced a sleeper coach service between Liverpool and Newcastle using single-deck Guy Coaches fitted with twelve bunks. The following year saw a service inaugurated between Liverpool/Manchester and London by Land Liners Ltd using two six-wheel Guy double-deck chassis with bodywork by

Liverpool Corporation purchased 38 FCX long-wheelbase chassis between 1927 and 1929, bodying all of them at its Edge Lane workshops. The first four, of which three are seen here, were double-deckers, the bodywork understandably having clear links to the undertaking's tramcar designs. They seated 70 as built, and were thus among the largest-capacity motor buses in the country at the time, though the figure was soon reduced to 62. The remainder were single-deckers, Liverpool having one of the largest fleets of 6-wheel single-deck buses in the country, but all its FCXs had been withdrawn by 1937.

Strachan & Brown. It is reported that a passenger on the inaugural service, on feeling sick in the lower deck, made his way to an upper booth where he was sick!

Such pioneering services were ahead of their time. It would take the advent of the motorway age in 1959, 30 years on, with vastly improved chassis and suspension design and of course improved roads to make such ideas feasible.

One of the best foreign chassis on the British market in the 'twenties was the Italian Lancia. It was very popular

Oldham Corporation also had both double- and single-deck FCX buses, all the twelve built in 1927 having bodywork by Roe, including three single-deckers as shown here, originally seating 39, but later reduced to 37 before withdrawal in 1935. This view shows the style of radiator used on most of the earlier FCX chassis, larger and more angular than that on the BX series.

A further change in radiator style came in 1929, when the pattern shown here was introduced, though it did not reflect more than minor changes elsewhere in design. It was very broad and slightly more rounded than the 1927-8 style — when fitted to a normal-control vehicle, as here, it seemed to dominate the whole front of the bus. This was one of 30 two-axle single-deckers with 25-seat Guy bodywork supplied to Birmingham Corporation in 1929-30. The chassis were thus of the rare 'plain' C-type, though retrospectively sometimes called Guy Conquest models, adopting the single-deck type name applied to later examples of this series from 1931. The C-range chassis had Guy side-valve 6-cylinder engines of 6.8 or 7.6 litres.

with the passenger carrying industry because of the good design and for its time, high performance. One man who recognised the qualities of Vincenzo Lancia's designs was Thomas Henry Barton who modified the Lancia chassis to his own requirements. Thomas H. Barton founded his famous bus company in 1897. He was not only a great character but also a very inventive engineer.

L. Gardner & Sons Ltd of Patricroft, Manchester were known for their marine engines at this time. They had produced a reliable diesel engine in the shape of the 5.6-litre 4L2.

Thomas H. Barton persuaded a reluctant engine manufacturer to supply him with a 4L2 unit; this was fitted into a Lancia-Barton which successfully entered service during March 1930.

The success of this conversion was not lost on many in the heavy vehicle industry and in particular Guy Motors, which would again show the industry that they had lost none of their inventiveness. Very little

Below: Hull Corporation took six FCX chassis in 1929, again with the new style of radiator. They had bodywork built by Brush, but it seems that they were to Roe design, having both the general appearance and many detail features of contemporary Roe products – Brush was adept at such work. The vehicle, with five bay body, appears to be on the shorter-length chassis.

In 1930 the company took a lead from T. H. Barton and offered a Gardner diesel engine as an option in the 4 and 6-wheel Invincible bus chassis, as well as on the four and 6-wheel goods chassis. The latter were known as the Warrior and Goliath, designed for six and eleven ton payloads. The combination of Guy and Gardner, though very small at first, was an enduring one and the company offered the famous Manchester built engines in its vehicles until the end of production.

Guy's efforts on the military front centred on a 6 x 6 design in 1930 followed by an 8 x 8 design in 1931. Despite difficult trading conditions the company was still exporting vehicles.

The year 1930 saw South Africa put its first trolleybus into operation. Guy Motors built up an excellent export business with South Africa but wrong decisions made in 1955 regarding the South Africa market were eventually a major cause of the company going into receivership in 1961.

Two events in 1931 would have a great effect on the British motor industry for many years to come and eventually on Guy Motors. One was the introduction by General Motors of the Bedford commercial vehicle that would by the 1950s see many of the smaller traditional commercial vehicle and bus manufacturers either in trouble or out of business. SS (forerunner of Jaguar), also established that year, would have a similar effect on the car market – buying Daimler in 1960 to gain extra factory space and some would say, respectability, as well as the best selling rear-engine bus of the time and in 1961, Guy Motors.

By 1932 the depression was at its worst but the government of the day rejected the expansionist methods that would be used later, successfully, by Franklin D. Roosevelt in America. Politicians seemed indifferent to the situation here in Britain, while in Germany Adolf Hitler and the National Socialist Party were showing alarming tendencies.

It was against this worrying background that Sydney Guy introduced the Wolf 2 ton range. The new range was launched, with a fanfare of publicity, by Sir Malcolm Campbell at a luncheon at the Guy works in May 1933.

Sir Malcolm, the great record breaker on land and water, was often used by companies to introduce new models, such was the prestige of his name.

Shortly after the Wolf came the 3/4 ton Vixen, with stronger springs and larger wheels and tyres. Both designs were powered by a Meadows 3.3-litre 4-cylinder engine and would prove popular with bus and coach operators as well as hauliers.

Photographed in August 1929, soon after delivery, is Birmingham Corporation No. 74, which was one of 30 similar machines. The chassis is a Guy Conquest, being the single-deck version of the Invincible double-decker. The imposing radiator is surmounted by an early example of the American Indian mascot. The high bonnet covered a large 6-cylinder petrol engine of 105 bhp. The sleek Guy body sat low on the chassis and carried 25 passengers. A front entrance with manual jack-knife doors was provided. Built originally for one-man bus work, they were returned to Guy Motors in 1931/2 for conversion to forward control, increasing the seating by seven.

Above: By 1930, Guy's 6-wheel motor bus era was fading fast. Hull's final batch of six FCX models delivered in the latter part of that year again had Brush bodywork to much the same style as the batch illustrated on page 36, splendid in retrospect but becoming dated-looking even when new. This time the bodies were of six-bay form and evidently longer. The radiator style had changed again, to a type to be standard on the heavier Guy models until 1932 and associated with the introduction of model names, in this case Invincible.

Below: South Lancashire Transport converted their tramways (excepting three miles) to trolleybus operation in 1930-33. The company purchased 30 Guy BTX trolleybuses in 1930/31. They were bodied by Roe with lowbridge layout and body styling clearly influenced by the then recently introduced Leyland Titan. Examples lasted until the closure of the trolleybus operation in 1958. When originally introduced in their striking livery of red and white with gold and black lining out, the SLT trolleybuses represented the best of British inter-urban transport.

Above: A 1930 advertisement for the 110 brake horse-power model FC6 Warrior. The two-axled model FC6 Warrior cost £995 and was only available in forward control form, giving 17ft bodyspace for a 6 ton payload which could be carried at 20 mph.

Below: The three-axled Goliath was a development of the Warrior but had both rear axles driven and an eight-speed gearbox. Designed for a twelve ton load, a 22ft-long body could be accommodated. The chassis cost £1,460 and was designated FCZ. If the Gardner 6LW engine was fitted the price was £1,895 and the designation changed to FDZ. The example shown in the photograph has a 22ft triple dropside body with a solid rear cab headboard and central vision aperture. The steel furniture (fittings) would have been supplied by Pinks of Sheffield who still supply coachbuilders today. The body frame would have been constructed in ash and set directly over the main chassis frame. Large U bolts would have held the structure in position. It is likely that the bodywork would have been made from parana pine using tongue and groove construction with oak square case flooring.

Above: A 1930 2-ton truck owned by Chambers & Marsh Ltd, timber merchants of Oldbury in the West Midlands. The narrow cab and the support attached to the scuttle and wing enabled long lengths of timber to be carried.

Below: Guy still produced the 15 cwt model in 1932. This pair were among the last to be made. They joined an all-Guy fleet operated by a Lancashsire pharmeceutical manufacturer who praised the economy and reliability of Guy's products. These two examples exhibit typical construction features of this period. For example, the roofs were constructed in $1\frac{1}{4}$ x $\frac{3}{16}$ softwood slats. The slats were covered with layers of white duck canvas soaked in white primer and stretched over the softwood framework. The side shutter is also of wood construction with pieces of pine $1\frac{1}{8}$in x $\frac{3}{8}$in attatched to a twin row of continuous steel hinges and fixed to a top pole.

Above: Derby Corporation bought 76 BTX trolleybuses between 1932 and 1937, becoming one of Guy's biggest customers for the type. Most had 56-seat bodywork built by Brush to its characteristic sloping-profile interpretation of the piano-front outline, as evident in this June 1946 scene outside the town's railway station.

Below: South Lancashire Transport's second batch of Guy trolleybuses were of the BTtwo-axle model, again bodied by Roe of Leeds. Undoubtedly a first-class investment, many lasted in service until the end of the system's existence though some body rebuilding had taken place after the war. Both these and the earlier batch had a feature which endeared them to local enthusiasts – the lack of traction batteries. When the 'Whit Walks' (a traditional northern custom) took place, or when roadworks required diversions, these vehicles were powered by trailing jump leads hooked onto the overhead wires and often four or five vehicles' length long. The Health & Safety Executive would surely have put a stop to such operation had it been in existence in those halcyon days!

Above: The start of a new range came in 1933 with the Wolf 2/3 tonner. Whilst using the same 3.3-litre 4-cylinder Meadows engine as the ON series, they were lighter and in theory more economical to run. This forward-control van was bought by a Cheshire firm in 1934. Note the radiator now slopes rearwards.

Below: The Wolf was also available in normal-control form. The Leeds and Wakefield Brewery took delivery of this drop-sided lorry in 1935. Although supplied by their local distributor, it was for some reason registered in West Bromwich. The unladen weight was 1 ton 19 cwt.

The Road Traffic Act 1930, as well bringing in a system of bus route licensing, introduced new national dimensional standards which came into effect from 1st January 1932. Up to this date, varying local restrictions, particularly on length, had been in force, sometimes very restrictive, though a few operators had been free to produce very long vehicles by the standards of the time. On the other hand, the new limit of 26ft for two-axle double-deck buses, allowing seating capacity of up to 56 or so, helped to encourage the choice of such vehicles in preference to the more complex three-axle types, though trolleybus operators, with less restrictive weight limits, still tended to favour the 6-wheeler.

Among goods vehicles, the 'thirties brought new trends, again influenced by the effects of weight restrictions. Goods vehicles of up to 50cwt unladen weight were allowed to travel at up to 30mph, whereas those weighing more continued to be restricted to 20mph. This tended to encourage the use of light vehicles, such as the Guy Wolf and Vixen, though the main beneficiaries tended to be the lower-priced makes, notably Bedford. Guy fought back with more advanced specifications, the Wolf and Vixen being offered with a Dorman-Ricardo 4DS 3.05-litre 4-cylinder diesel engine, though few were sold.

The most famous of all Guy models is undoubtedly the Arab, introduced in 1933. It was promoted as the first bus chassis designed for a diesel engine, the Gardner LW range introduced two years earlier being chosen. In fact, the Arab inherited a good deal of its general chassis design from the previous FC type, latterly called the Invincible. Indeed, an FC-type demonstrator (UK 8047) that was operated by Birmingham Corporation as its 97 from December 1929, and reported to have run latterly with a Gardner 5LW 5-cylinder diesel engine, was returned to Guy at the end of 1933, emerging rebuilt as an Arab. It had received a 6-cylinder 6LW power unit and a new Metro-Cammell body and rejoined the Birmingham fleet early in 1934, taking up the number of that undertaking's solitary 6-wheel Guy, withdrawn the previous year. Some all-new Arab buses were already in service elsewhere by then.

In addition to the diesel engine, which may account for the FD model designation, there was a further new radiator design, of similar outline to the previous type, but with a less-massive surround. Features from earlier types were the double-plate clutch and amidships-mounted four-speed gearbox. This had the usual H-gate gear lever postions as pioneered by Packard on their model A as far back as 1899, but with gear positions opposite to normal. This latter was not unique, but did not endear itself to drivers used to the more usual arrangement.

On the other hand, the vacuum-hydraulic brakes were a modern feature, performing well, and the Marles steering

Among the first Arab FD48 buses built were a pair with centre-entrance English Electric bodywork for Blackpool Corporation, supplied in 1933 alongside a batch of Leyland Titan TD3 which were also among the first of their type. This view emphasises the length of bonnet needed for the 6LW engine, the front bulkhead being set well back behind the front mudguard. The Arabs were sold after only five years, though they saw further service with a Scottish independent operator. The TD3 buses ran for sixteen years, admittedly in an almost all-Leyland fleet during that period.

was described as light in contemporary reports. The tranmission line, and hence the differential of the worm-drive rear axle, were offset to the right rather than the left as more usual, a feature shared with Crossley buses of the period.

The early single-deck Arab was available in two lengths, 26ft and 27ft 6in, known as FD32 and FD35 respectively, and both with a choice of the 4-cylinder 4LW giving 68bhp or the 85bhp 5LW. The double-decker, originally FD48, could have ether the 5LW or the 6LW which gave 102bhp. There was still a three-axle model, FDX60, aimed largely at overseas users.

Despite its general mechanical design being similar to the much-respected wartime Arab introduced in 1942, early Arab sales were sluggish, admittedly in a difficult market, and quite a number of the total, which seems barely to have reached 50 by 1936, had shorter lives than most of their contemporaries, sometimes markedly so, suggesting that there may have been some design fault, perhaps with the frame, since this was the main feature which was altered on the durable wartime model.

The Arab FD was by definition a forward-control model, but when Burton on Trent required four normal-control buses in 1934 two of the vehicles supplied were Guys to Arab design, including the provision of Gardner 4LW engines, but were quoted as BB models, the chassis numbers being prefixed thus. The others were an AEC Ranger and a Leyland Lioness, both also being 4-cylinder. They were among the last heavy-duty normal-control buses supplied to a British municipal fleet, and the conservative approach of this undertaking was emphasised by the use of railway-style oil side lamps. The following year's delivery of ten single-deckers were forward-control Arab FD models, again 4LW-powered. At that date, Burton used only single-deck buses because of the numerous bridges then in the area. Nine more FD models were supplied in 1936, Burton continuing as a regular Arab purchaser until 1961, though latterly double-deck.

Burton on Trent was a regular customer for Guy buses from the 'twenties to 1961 and these two were photographed when new in 1934 and 1935 respectively. Both carry Brush bodywork and the deep radiator gives the normal control version in particular an extremely impressive appearance. Forward visibility for the driver was perhaps less impressive on this model.

At the Olympia Show of 1935 the company introduced a Cotal gearbox. In the Cotal epicyclic gearbox, the frictional bands were immobilised by electric magnets to provide the different gear ratios. Although the design was thoroughly tested and used by quality French car marques such as Delahaye into the post-war period it never made any headway against the British alternative, the Wilson gearbox. Guy's rival Daimler had introduced the Wilson box, coupled to its fluid flywheel, at the beginning of the decade. This combination was also adopted by AEC and later by Guy.

The Warrior and Goliath models finished production in 1934. Launched at a very difficult time, the Guy heavies had not been a success despite an interesting specification. This was not a dissimilar situation to that at Bedfords when they launched the TM range – they were not thought of as a builder of heavy commercials. In Guy's case the situation was compounded by the economic depression.

This was a very difficult time for Sydney Guy and his company. Earlier, in March 1932 production of the Star car ceased; commercial vehicle production having stopped a year prior to that.

The Star car was quoted in Buyers Guide Lists up to 1935. Any unsold cars and parts had been purchased by McKenzie & Denley of Birmingham.

The Wolf and Vixen models were now joined by the Otter and the Fox range. The Otter was rated as a six-tonner and was competitively priced at £400. Thanks to its lightweight chassis, it offered a greater payload than many rivals. For an additional £65 one could purchase the Fox which in effect was a six-wheel version of the Otter.

The Wolf, Vixen and Otter ranges would find many loyal customers over the coming years. Many household names purchased the Wolf and Vixen right up to the latter's demise in 1961. Among these were Chivers, Ever Ready, British Oxygen, CWS, Harrods, Lewis, Lyons and Whiteways Cider. From Pickfords Removals there was a yearly order for around 100 Vixens in post-war years.

Despite the disappointments with cars, heavy-duty trucks and buses during this period, the trolleybus market sales remained steady, the BTX three-axle chassis meeting with wide approval.

South Lancs took 46 vehicles equipped with Roe lowbridge bodywork during the period 1930-1933. Wolverhampton Corporation took 65 vehicles between 1930 and 1936. These were fitted with a variety of bodies by Beadle, Brush, Dodson, Guy and MCW.

The company was favoured with orders from Derby between 1932 and 1937 for 75 vehicles with 56-seat bodies supplied by Dodson, and Weymann and Brush.

The Hastings Tramways fleet consisted mainly, up to 1945, of BTX35 single-deckers with central-entrance bodies by Ransomes, Sims and Jeffries and 10 BTX60 double-deckers dating from 1928-9.

By 1935 there were still two million people out of work. After 1932 there was a slow but steady recovery in the economy but inflation was the great worry of the Governments of the 'thirties. This was held in check by a large pool of unemployed people – a situation which gave stable prices but at a high social cost. For many, a stable job was paramount. The bus industry benefited greatly with a steady flow of applicants. Many of these men had known the rigours of military discipline and as a result they made excellent adverts for their companies with their smart appearance and punctual habits.

In Wolverhampton there was always a pool of skilled labour eager to fill any vacancy that occurred at Guy's Fallings Park works. Although Sydney Guy's industrial policy on personnel matters was in advance of most competitors, anyone caught producing shoddy work would be fired on the spot.

By the middle of the decade there was a belated recognition by the authorities that the situation in Germany could become very unpleasant. Adolf Hitler had seized the reins of power. It was time for Britain to start preparing for the unthinkable again.

A handsome Star Planet Coupé of 1931. With a 6-cylinder engine of 20 hp (RAC) rating, four-wheel hydraulic jacking and servo brakes offering '1941 motoring luxury and economy' the Planet was a nice car at the wrong time.

In 1935 Guy Motors was invited to take part in Army trials held at Llangollen in North Wales. As a result of submitting a design that not only met the requirements of the specification laid down by the authorities but performed well in the trials, the company was asked to produce 150 vehicles in 1936.

With a payload of 15 cwt and a short wheelbase, the Ant ran on low pressure tyres of large section. The design used flat sheet metal sections, thus helping to reduce costs all round. In appearance the Ant showed a similarity to the later standard Canadian military designs which were mounted on Chevrolet and Ford chassis.

The year 1937 saw a 4x4 version known as the Quad Ant. It was ordered by the War Department for use as a gun tractor. An all-steel, fully enclosed body was fitted, with seating provided for the driver, a commander and four crew. There were lockers for ammunition, with more carried in the limber towed behind the tractor. A crash bar was fitted across the radiator grille on to which winch cable could be hooked. Most Quad Ants went to Field Artillery units pulling seventeen or 25-pounder guns, apart from one batch which towed anti-tank guns.

In 1943 the War Department placed its final order for this model. A batch of 700 was produced for use as General Service trucks.

Also in 1937, a forward-control version of the Ant was produced for the War Department. It featured a longer wheel base and incorporated a dynamo in the drive line. Known as the model PE, it saw service as a mobile generator for powering searchlights. The three-axle FBAX was used for similar work. Due to the development of

Above: The Otter was added to the goods range, designed to carry a 6-ton payload and with suitable bodywork, it weighed under 50 cwt, enabling it to run at 30 mph. The engine was the 58 bhp 3.7-litre petrol unit. The vehicle is fitted with India tyres, which, in the second half of the 'thirties, had a red line around the circumference of the tyre. The idea was revived in the 'sixties by some American tyre manufacturers, for tyres fitted to high performance cars of the period.

Below: To meet the War Department's requirements for a vehicle to carry 15 cwt payload across country, Guy produced the Ant. This was based on Wolf and Vixen components but having large wide section tyres to give better ground clearance and traction off the road. This is an early production example.

Above: Southampton Corporation had been a customer for Guy buses since 1926, when three model-B 26-seaters had entered the fleet, followed by three OND 18-seat buses in 1927 and a further seventeen Bs were placed in service between then and 1930, all of these having bodywork built by the operator. Then there was a gap until 1934, during which Thornycroft was the main supplier, but twelve Guy Arab FD double-deckers with Gardner 5LW engines and Park Royal bodywork were supplied between 1934 and 1936, including the 1935 example with metal-framed body shown above. Here the Arab was well liked and these buses remained in service until 1949-51. It seems quite probable that further Arab buses might have followed, had not the Guy works been so busy with military contracts, and Leyland supplied most of the undertaking's needs until 1939. However, one Invincible demonstrator dating from 1931 was acquired in 1936 and ran until 1946. Wartime Arab buses were followed by a large post-war fleet supplied in 1946-54.

Below: Newcastle Corporation began trolleybus operation in October 1935, the initial fleet of 30 being split equally between AEC, Guy and Karrier chassis, the three makes sharing later prewar orders, though not equally. This publicity photograph of five of the first Guy BTX models was taken near Central Station. The vehicles were 30ft long and had 80hp motors with regenerative control. Metro-Cammell built the bodywork to a pattern, very modern-looking at the time, which was to remain the undertaking's standard for several years, with rear entrance, front exit and 60-seat capacity. Three more similar vehicles arrived in December 1936, ten in 1937 and a final ten in 1938, in which year there were also one BTX with Roe body (exhibited at the Earls Court Show in 1937), and one with Northern Coachbuilders body.

Above: Rotherham Corporation No. 33 (ET 9618) was one of a batch of seven 6-wheelers (BTX), dating from 1937, with a Cravens 39-seat centre-entrance body, and photographed on 8th May 1949. Rotherham was one of very few operators who required single-deck trolleybuses.

Below: Rotherham Corporation No. 62, (ET9233) was one of seven single-deck Guy BT four-wheel trolleybuses purchased by the corporation in 1937, again with Cravens centre-entrance bodies. Also photographed on the 8th May 1949, No. 62 shows the corporation's stylish art deco livery to good effect.

One of the latest
GUY TROLLEY BUSES
for WOLVERHAMPTON CORPORATION

BATTERY MANOEUVRES

An additional feature is incorporated in the Guy 4-wheel double-deck Trolley Buses operated by Wolverhampton Corporation. The vehicles are equipped with two 24-volt batteries, these are connected in parallel for lighting, but if required for battery manoeuvring they are connected in series giving 48-volts which produces a source of power by which the vehicles can be driven for a distance of 2 or 3 miles **without the use of the overhead power lines.** This feature is a great advantage—for instance, should a driver want to take his vehicle into the depot, or for manoeuvring in the depot, it is possible to do so without the assistance of the overhead wires.

A few Corporations who run fleets of GUY Trolley Buses :—

Wolverhampton -	89
Newcastle-on-Tyne	13
Derby - - -	72
Hastings - -	58
South Lancs. -	46

Ask for illustrated literature

GUY MOTORS LTD., Wolverhampton. 'Phone : Fallings Park 31421
London Sales and Service : Porteus Road, Paddington, W. 2. - - 'Phone : Padd 4492

An advertisement placed in 1936 when the Wolverhampton trolleybus was new.

GUYS FOR LIFE

Illustrated is a GUY "VIXEN" 3/4 tonner recently supplied to The Rustless Iron Co. Ltd.

21st REPEAT ORDER FOR GUY VEHICLES!

The Rustless Iron Co. Ltd., Keighley, who operate a large fleet of GUY vehicles recently took delivery of their 21st repeat order. They—like many other discriminating buyers—economise with Guys by their longer life and lower running cost.

Write for Illustrated Literature to:—

GUY MOTORS LTD. **WOLVERHAMPTON**
LONDON SALES AND SERVICE — PORTEUS ROAD PADDINGTON W. 2.

An advertisement placed in 1938.

radar, which was found to be more accurate in locating aircraft, the final batches of the PE and FBAX were produced in 1939. From 1936 until 1941 civilian Guy vehicles were only produced in small numbers. Arab bus production virtually ceased, except for a final batch to pre-war style for Burton in 1940-41, though BTX and BT trolleybuses continued to be built, notably for Wolverhampton, Newcastle and Rotherham.

In 1938 the company brought out the first rear-engined, four-wheel drive, all welded armoured car. Utilising many of the units from the Ant/Quad Ant range, the all-welded armoured car was manufactured in the face of every kind of opposition from the War Office and Ministry of Supply who claimed that it was impossible to weld armoured plate without cracking occurring. This was despite evidence to the contrary where, according to Robin Guy, the War Office knew that such welding could be done.

The same officials claimed that wheeled vehicles would be too vulnerable in actual war. Sydney Guy was offered a title in the hope that this would silence him but he declined the honour. Several hundred Guy armoured cars were then built. However, due to the demand for the vehicle and the fact that the company was unable to produce it in the numbers required, the design was given to Humber and the patented process made available to the Government for the duration of the war.

It has been estimated that Guy's invention saved the country one million pounds on tank production alone due to the elimination of the machining of the Homogeneous

Hard Plate. In human terms the number of casualties caused by rivet heads flying around inside the vehicles was greatly reduced. Vehicles constructed using Guy's patent method were totally water-proof and were thus able to 'wade' to a considerable depth.

Official circles recognised the importance of Guy's development when, soon after the war the company received an award from the Royal Commission on Awards to Inventors.

Sydney Guy was not alone in having problems convincing the authorities of the soundness of his ideas. During the inter-war years Liddel Hart wrote several works on the vital role that the tank would play in modern warfare. The German authorities took notice whilst the British did nothing until almost the eleventh hour. As a result, by 1940 the German Army was sweeping across continental Europe. The same story was to be repeated in many other fields.

A telling example of thinking in Government circles was the comparative spending in 1929 between fodder for horses (£607,000) and petrol for tanks (£72,000).

Small Guy buses and coaches were part of the scene in Llandudno for many years. Setting down passengers outside the White Court Hotel on 14th April 1954 is JC 9736. This Wolf was one of a pair bought new by Llandudno UDC in 1949. Powered by Meadows 4EL (22½hp) 4-cylinder petrol engines, these two 20-seat buses were bodied by Barnard. Having continued to work in this North Wales holiday resort into the 1970s, this suitably vintage-looking vehicle was guaranteed a place in preservation.

Left: The FBAX of mid-'twenties basic design was a double drive 6-wheeled chassis used by the army for a wide variety of duties including mobile workshops and with a generator, to power searchlights. In common with many Army vehicles built in pre-war times, some retained the open cab, the frames for the canvas hood being seen here.

Below: Guy Motors pioneered the welding of bullet-proof armour plate and used it in the building of the armoured car. This used the same mechanical units as the Quad-Ant but with the engine mounted at the rear. A column is seen going through a country village during the Second World War.

Above: A 1927 BB 3-ton coal truck still hard at work fifteen years later. The vehicle was operated by W. B. Anderson of Galashiels, Scotland. The body is very typical of its type, with a subframe constructed in ash. The longitudinal ladder frame chassis has transverse cross members spaced at intervals of 2ft. Tapered flooring was used to make the coal bags lean towards the centre of the bed, thus increasing load safety. It is likely that this vehicle was put to alternative use at times as there is a tubular steel tilt frame fixed to the rear bulkhead.

Below: Civilian vehicles were still being produced in small numbers in the late 'thirties. This 1937 Wolf with optional small wheels gave a very low platform height making it ideal for local delivery work, and a dual passenger seat enabled a three-man crew to be carried for handling beer barrels. Note the masked headlamps and white markings on the front wings, indicating that both these photographs were taken during the Second World War.

This wartime Guy advertisement is interesting in showing how it subtley glamorises the utility body – Birmingham's livery was doubtless deliberately chosen in the hope of attracting custom from that quarter.

As we have seen in the previous chapter Guy's survival in the 'thirties had largely been thanks to the War Office orders, tardy though those orders might have been in relation to the war effort. Now, in 1939, all civilian vehicle production virtually stopped with the arrival of hostilities.

Government reaction had been over cautious and before long it became apparent that a shortage of buses was developing, making the movement of essential personnel on wartime production difficult, if not impossible, in some parts of the country. Clearly the ban was counter productive and accordingly a new strategy was devised.

After the cancellation of the searchlight vehicle order, due to the introduction of radar, the Ministry of Transport asked Guy Motors to produce a chassis suitable for double-deck bodywork. The specification was drawn up on 5th September 1941, with a prototype ready by 31st March 1942. The Guy Arab utility double-decker bus was based on its namesake of 1933 but aluminium components were replaced by cast iron.

The design gained an excellent reputation for durability and it is true to say that the success of the Arab utility not only saved Guy Motors from possible closure by the 1950s but established the company as a leading producer of bus and coach chassis in the post-war world. An estimated 2,750 wartime Arabs were built, taking the marque to many new customers. Production of Arabs in the 'thirties had been minimal, barely 60 being built between the introduction of the model in 1934 and the cessation of build in 1939. Many operators ordering Guys after the war

had either tried the marque in the 'thirties and given it up, or had never operated a Guy at all. The wartime Arab made many friends in the operating world.

Originally both Leyland and Guy were going to be involved in the production of utility double-decker buses. Two initial batches of 500 vehicles from each manufacturer were planned but in the event it was to be Guy Motors which produced the majority of utility double-deck chassis, with Leyland's production being concentrated elsewhere.

This was because of the Lancashire company's involvement in tank and military vehicle production and the fact that it had become bogged down with problems concerning the cooling system of the Rolls Royce Meteor engine when installed in the Crusader tank. The Meteor engine was a variation of the famous Merlin aero engine, minus supercharger. Rolls Royce and Leyland problems came about because although the Crusader was the latest tank in production in 1940, its 330 hp Liberty engine, which dated from World War I, was partially exposed on the outside of the tank. The Meteor engine had to be totally enclosed and developed 600 hp. It is said that Leyland pulled out of the development stage in despair at ever solving the problem of overheating.

This lowbridge Duple-bodied Arab utility of 1942 was used by Guy Motors in their publicity and advertising of the period. The vehicle was the fifth to be produced, and was probably the first to be painted in the livery of Red & White Services Ltd. In the post-war period the Red & White name became synonymus with both Duple and Guy.

Above: Nottingham City Transport No. 306 started life in Hastings & District's fleet as No. 47, a 1928/29 Guy BTX single-decker. It carried a Ransomes centre-entrance 32-seat body of suitably vintage appearance with high body line and triple lifeguard rails. Photographed on a dull wet August day in 1943 at Wollaton Park, Nottingham, it shows wartime white painted lifeguard rails, mudguards and headlamp masks. The trolley retrieval pole was carried in holes in the nearside roof!

Below: A Guy model CX normal-control double-deck bus of 1929 vintage in service with Leicester City Transport during the second war. Leicester bought 23 examples of the model CX with Brush 56-seat bodies. Because of wartime regulations the nearside headlight is masked and part of the legal lettering has been painted over.

With the aid of further Government funds and a strong belief in Henry Royce's dictum "There is no such thing as an insoluble problem", Rolls Royce engineers carried on alone and solved the cooling system problem. The end result was the Cromwell tank.

Manufacturers of buses were then instructed by the Ministry of Supply to build from components which were already in stock. Such vehicles were referred to as 'unfrozen' but the numbers produced – about 450 – were a drop in the ocean compared with what was required nationwide.

Guy Motors therefore became the only manufacturer of utility double-deck chassis until December 1942 when it was announced that the Daimler company was resuming production with a new chassis for double-deck buses, the CWG5.

The Daimler Works had been badly damaged in the air raids on Coventry in 1940 and 1941, and, as a result, the supply of Daimler chassis ceased earlier than those of its rivals. The new Daimler was assembled in Wolverhampton at a factory requisitioned from Courtaulds by the Ministry of Supply. Wolverhampton was now the centre of double-deck chassis production in Britain, with Luton the centre for single-deck production on the Bedford OWB chassis. Trolleybus production was also concentrated in Wolverhampton during the war years since the Sunbeam and Karrier companies had been bought-up by the Rootes Group some years earlier in 1934 and 1935. The standard wartime utility trolleybus could be badged as either Karrier or Sunbeam, though after 1948 when Guy Motors purchased Sunbeam all trolleybuses were badged as Sunbeam.

Mechanically, the original Arab was claimed to be the first British bus that was only available with a diesel engine. The wartime version offered sophisticated engine mounts which incorporated rubber with steel springs, which was an advance on pre-war designs. The standard engine was the Gardner 5LW unit, with the 6LW unit only available to operators with hilly routes. Initially the 6LW engined versions were very much in the minority. In terms of appearance they were easily recognisable by the longer bonnet, resulting in the radiator shell being mounted further forward and the mudguards having a lip on the leading edge in order to harmonise with the radiator shell. This simple guide was to disappear with the decision to mount all radiators forward, thus allowing either engine to be fitted within the same basic layout.

By December 1944 the two thousandth Arab Utility chassis had been built. The chassis frame was different from the Arab of the early 1930s, however, and the profile was almost identical to the Leyland Titan TD7 of the 1939-41 period. This was probably a result of the original plan whereby Guy and Leyland were both to have been the two manufacturers of utility double-deck bus chassis.

The transmission of the wartime Arab was a fine piece of vintage machinery, the origins of which went back to

A Park Royal-bodied Arab I in service with London Transport, GLF 657 entered service in February 1943, and was withdrawn in 1951. When the vehicle was overhauled in the early post-war years the cast iron radiator was replaced by the later aluminium design as seen in this photograph which was taken outside Victoria Station.

the late 1920s. Even the double plate clutch was rather dated by the early 1940s and the unusual about-face gear shift pattern was retained. What mattered was that, despite its somewhat vintage specification in some areas, the wartime Arab showed itself to be an excellent design. In 1944 Bristol resumed the production of chassis on a very small scale and by the summer of that year certain restrictions were slightly relaxed, allowing, amongst other things, aluminium sheet to be reintroduced for bodywork. Towards the end of 1944 upholstered seats were again allowed – quite a relief for many after the discomfort of the war years when slatted wooden seats had been the order of the day.

With 'Victory in Europe' in 1945, standards of construction and design gradually improved. Nevertheless the distinctive utility buses from Bedford, Bristol, Daimler and Guy, with their angular bodywork, could still be seen in parts of Britain up to the 1960s.

Despite the numbers of bus chassis produced for what was a relatively small company, Guy Motors from 1941 also built the Vixant truck in limited numbers. Designed for essential users, the chassis was rated at 4 tons and based on the late 'thirties Vixen. The very angular cab used pressings from the Ant range for its front end.

Production of the civilian Wolf and Vixen ranges was resumed in 1946. The designs were based on the pre-war model but with styling improvements.

Continued on page 65

Above: A long wheelbase Vix-Ant with a van body for carrying confectionery, delivered to a Staffordshire bakers in 1943. The Meadows 3.7-litre, 4-cylinder petrol engine with a four-speed gearbox was standard.

Below: An early medium wheelbase Vix-Ant with a 14ft-long dropsided body delivered to a Derbyshire rope manufacturer in 1942. Both headlamps had masks fitted allowing only a dim light, making driving extremely difficult at night.

Above: One of the problems frequently encountered after German air raids was the disruption in the supply of various essentials to the civilian population. One was water and to overcome this, a fleet of water tankers with tanks built by Thompson Bros (Bilston) Ltd, was purchased by subscriptions raised in America and presented to the British people. Fourteen are seen here at Fallings Park before delivery.

Below: The short wheelbase Vix-Ant 4-ton chassis was suitable for use as a tipper. To give maximum body length, an underfloor tipping gear was fitted. The customer must have been pleased with it as he bought more Guys in the 1950s.

Left: GYL 343 was photographed in largely original condition on 1st June 1953, having emigrated to Scotland and become E88 in the Highland Omnibus fleet. This bus was delivered new to London Transport in June 1945 as G 204. Park Royal built the body, which was to relaxed utility specification. The rear and front roof domes were rounded and beaten, the usual Park Royal exterior waist mouldings were omitted and moquette seats were fitted. The radiator shows the usual painted finish over the cast iron surround. The crease in the panel between the offside side light and the lower edge of the windscreen was a Park Royal identifying pattern.

Below: A brace of Arab IIs with consecutive registrations HRB 982/3 were numbers 22 and 23 in the fleet of Midland General. Delivered new in 1944, they were fitted with 6LW engines. They were photographed in Mount Street, Nottingham in August 1949, and look very smart in their operator's livery of blue and cream following repaint and bearing the elaborate garter crest on the side panels. The destination boxes have been modified and show the Midland General characteristic 'alpha numeric' route numbering system. Bodywork was by Northern Counties, who continued to use metal-framed construction on all their wartime bodies – doubtless contributing to their longer life than the productions of their rivals. Saloon window pans were radiused, which together with the metal framework, reduced movement on the body pillars.

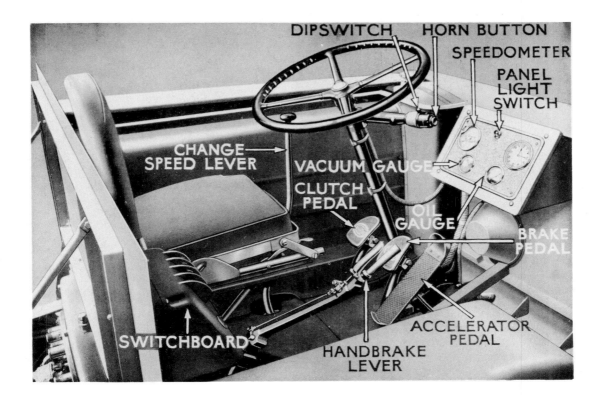

DIPSWITCH HORN BUTTON

SPEEDOMETER

PANEL LIGHT SWITCH

CHANGE SPEED LEVER

VACUUM GAUGE

CLUTCH PEDAL

OIL GAUGE

BRAKE PEDAL

SWITCHBOARD

ACCELERATOR PEDAL

HANDBRAKE LEVER

Below: Number 29 in the fleet of Green Bus Company of Rugeley, GKC 249, still looking tidy when photographed on 12th July 1959. One of eighteen Guy Arab originally delivered to Liverpool Corporation during the war, interestingly, it was fitted with a pre-war body intended for an AEC Regent. The frames were supplied by Weymanns, and LCT panelled and finished the bodies in its Edge Lane works. The high scuttle, small angled windscreen, destination boxes and sloping front give a suitably vintage appearance.

Above: The wartime Arab chassis was by no means lacking in refinement, even though the 'utility' aspect was emphasised in line with wartime Government propaganda. Indeed the cab was not as spartan as that of some pre-war makes – this view from the service manual even shows the provision of a clock. The driving position was quite comfortable, with steering column more mildly raked than the pre-war version. The provision of quite an effective flexible mounting for the engine kept the level of vibration and noise down for passengers. However, performance was hardly sprightly with the standard Gardner 5LW five-cylinder engine on a vehicle which was often a ton or so heavier than typical pre-war double-deckers – in addition, buses were usually heavily laden because of wartime restriction on services. It is significant that the manual apologises in advance for this, stating that Guy would have preferred to fit the the 6-cylinder unit as standard, though supply restrictions did not allow this.

LICHFIELD

GKC249

Above: East Yorkshire Motor Services No. 408 (GRH 192) was an Arab II and displays the extended bonnet snout resulting from the lengthened chassis to accommodate either a 5LW or larger 6LW Gardner engine. The upturned front wings are a further identifying feature. This body was one of seventeen special highbridge bodies built by Roe to the unique style required by EYMS to pass under the Beverley Bar. The angular corner lines of the non-beaten roof dome are particularly noticeable in this June 1950 view at Scarborough.

Below: Seen outside Mansfield Garage in June 1952 is East Midland D37 (GNN 437) which is an Arab II fitted with a 5LW engine. Lowbridge bodywork was by Charles H. Roe and the bus wears the old and very attractive East Midland livery of beige, cream and brown.

Above: Churchill's victory sign is prominent on the board in front of the 1000th wartime Guy Arab chassis, posed with a group of works staff including a lady driver who may well have been waiting to take it to the bodybuilders. In the background can be seen a line of the Vix-Ants, which, as mentioned in the text would be produced in small batches.

Below: The Arab II continued in production into 1946, when this example entered service with Young's Bus Service of Paisley. It had a 6LW engine and the Northern Counties body was the final derivative of that firm's utility style, becoming quite attractively styled with the return of curved outlines. This fleet passed to Western SMT, in whose service the vehicle is seen at Dumfries in 1960.

Above: Short wheelbase Vix-Ant, carrying a Derby-type refuse collection body, for a Welsh municipality. Whilst the cabs for the Ant and the Vix-Ant were similar, some Vix-Ants had a peaked bonnet.

Below: An early post-war Vixen 4-ton tipper went to a local engineering firm. It had a Guy cab and a body with Pilot underfloor tipping gear. The 10ft 7¾in wheelbase chassis and cab cost £615.00, the tipping gear £79 10s 0d and the 7 cu yd wooden body £115.00.

Facing page: Publicity line-up pictures of wartime utility Guy Arab buses were used quite extensively by the company to build up the image of the firm as a major manufacturer, though the buses had been supplied under wartime arrangements which gave the operator little choice. Bournemouth Corporation's fleet of eight, all dating from 1943, is seen towards the end of the war, still in drab livery, and still with masked headlamps. The four with Park Royal bodies (3-5th and 7th from left) were all Arab I 6-cylinder models. The remainder were Arab II models with Weymann bodywork. The post-war careers of wartime Guy buses varied considerably. Of the above Bournemouth buses, three of the Park Royal batch were still in the fleet 20 years later, with original bodywork, though benefitting from major rebuild in the operator's workshops. Two of the Weymann batch had gone, but of the two surviving, one, FRU 223, seen on the right of the picture as No. 39, had been drastically rebuilt as an open-topped single-decker and is seen here, renumbered 16.

An important change made in the specification of Arab II chassis in the summer of 1945 was the replacement of the old-type double-plate clutch and sliding-mesh gearbox with single-plate clutch and a newly-designed gearbox, with constant-mesh on all forward speeds (including first gear, unusual at that date) and a gate of conventional layout, in place of the reversed style previously charcteristic of the model. At once, the main source of driver complaint was eliminated, gear changes becoming less laborious and the noticeable whirring sounds from the old-style clutch as it was disengaged twice during the slow changes ceased to be evident to the passenger. The gear lever was fitted with a red knob to inform drivers that the new gearbox was fitted. Oddly enough, the new gearbox was slightly noisier than the old, which had been unusually quiet, but the whine now evident when indirect gears were in use was plesantly mellow in tone.

With the gradual return to the use of aluminium in bus construction, a worthwhile reduction in weight was gained on the early post-war Arabs.

War can never be a good thing but the developments which can be funded out of military budgets often benefit the community in a way which would not otherwise be possible. There can be no question that the post-war bus industry benefitted from Guy being awarded the wartime double-deck chassis contract, and, as already averred, the company itself was almost certainly saved from demise in the 'forties by the Arab production. Such was the volume of Arab production that once the order for Ants placed in 1942 had been completed the whole of the factory output, apart from small numbers of Vix-Ants already mentioned, was devoted to bus chassis building. How things had changed from the pre-war scene at Fallings Park.

In the next chapter we shall see how Guy capitalised on the sucess of its wartime Arab in a peacetime world.

In order to produce the large numbers of components required in the years between 1939 and 1945, the company offered teachers and senior pupils in the Wolverhampton area the chance to do warwork in the holidays. The scheme was extended so that in term time part-time women helpers could be employed during the day, with their places taken by professional and business men in the evenings. Over 1,000 people answered the first advertisement.

Judge Caporn, a local County Court Judge, was an early and enthusiastic volunteer. He served for almost four years and is creditied with helping to make the scheme such a success. Amongst other tasks, the new recruits were employed on the assembly of jigs for trucks for the military.

The long hours under blackout conditions and artificial light created health problems for some employees, so Guy Motors introduced sun-ray equipment in the works clinic. Medical staff were on hand to give treatment as required and, subject to the firm's doctor's approval, all employees were encouraged to take advantage of a sun-ray course free of charge.

The original utility Guy was unofficially known as the MkI. After the first 500 were produced, it was decided to standardise on the longer bonnet and distinctive front wing, as used originally on chassis fitted with the Gardner 6LW engine. In 1950 the 'Mk' was adopted for distinguishing between model types.

When the war finally finished in 1945 Guy had good reason to be proud of its contribution. Its employees had worked through the difficult years and produced more vehicles than at any time in the company's history. Over 2,700 bus chassis had been produced in some four years, compared with a mere 60 in the period from the introduction of the Arab in 1934 up to the cessation of manufacture in 1939. Military vehicles and munitions had been produced in quantity and the company would almost certainly not have survived had it not been for those orders. Now the task was to help rebuild the nation's transport system, but time was allocated to the construction and dedication of a garden which was opened within the works grounds to the memory of those servicemen and women who fell in the two world wars.

In 1946 a single-deck Arab chassis was introduced, to be produced alongside the double-deck version, and it was on this chassis that the lower bonnet was initially introduced, together with the return of a polished aluminium radiator.

The usual 5 and 6-cylinder Gardner diesel engines were offered on both chassis.

The lighter weight Wolf and Vixen models were re-introduced in 1947. The normal control Wolf was sold as suitable for 20-seat bodywork, with the forward control Vixen suitable for a 30-seat body. Their 4-cylinder petrol engines were the same as their pre-war counterparts. The radiator grille was modified so that it was now not unlike the MkII Arab, but with a central vertical strip.

Trolleybus production, as mentioned earlier, had been concentrated in Wolverhampton during the war years, with manufacture taking place at the Sunbeam Moorfield Works. Now, in 1947, Guy trolleybuses returned to the market, when the company produced 120 chassis. The following year saw Guy Motors purchase Sunbeam. Karrier production had been merged with Sunbeam before the war and all trolleybuses were subsequently marketed as Sunbeams and eventually all production was concentrated at Fallings Park from 1953.

As life returned to normal there was a large demand for buses and it was now that Guy felt the benefit of its wartime activities as customers old and new placed orders for Arabs. Bodybuilders were unable to meet the pent up demand as many operators decided to rebody older chassis and, seeing the opportunities, Guy began producing single-deck bus bodies along the lines of the then current Burlingham and BEFdesign.

Above left: This Arab III, FA 8422, was No. 33 in the fleet of Burton-on-Trent Corporation, who, as has been shown, were loyal Guy operators, building up a fleet of saloons and double-deckers. The 'High Street' scene is dated 7th August 1948. The bus was one of seven with Brush bodywork built in 1946. They had 5LW engines and thus had the 'Arab I'-style bonnet length standard on post-war single-deckers with this power unit.

Left: The post-war Guy lorry chassis were based on their pre-war counterparts but their appearance was improved by a new radiator with Guy cast in the top tank. One of the first was the 13ft 1¼in wheelbase Wolf.

Another similar wheelbase Wolf, but a normal control version, was delivered to Waring & Gillow in 1947. By this time larger headlamps were standard and, to aid the driver, a width indicator was fitted on the nearside wing.

The Vixen was popular as a pantechnicon. Delivered in 1948, this was an all Wolverhampton product as the body with integral cab was built by W. Robinson & Co. The 14ft 10¾in wheelbase chassis had a 16ft body.

This Guy Vixen/Otter with Wadhams bodywork was built in the early post-war period, and shows how the sloping dash supplied with the chassis was built into the bodywork. It is seen here in Birmingham at a rally of preserved vehicles in 1994.

CZ 8521, No. 157 was one of a batch of 70 three-axle BTX trolleybuses with 68-seat Harkness bodies locally built for Belfast Corporation, entering service between 1947 and 1950. Electrical equipment was by GEC. This smartly presented vehicle, pictured on 29th May 1952, wears the Corporation's red and white livery, with black lines marking the breaks of colour.

Wolverhampton 603 (FJW 603) was a BT two-axle chassis. It was one of a batch with Park Royal H54R bodies supplied in 1949. Parked alongside in this August 1951 view are two late 'thirties Austin saloons. The period 'Corporation Transport' multi-faced clock has unfortunately lost its hands.

Guy bodywork, based on a shell supplied by Park Royal, and the Meadows 6DC engine were features of Newport Corporation No. 8 (FDW 42), one of ten similar Arab III buses supplied in 1949. With this compact though powerful engine, the short bonnet was used for both double-and single-deck versions, and so the radiator did not project. Unfortunately the 6DC was troublesome and, as in some other cases, Gardner units were substituted later. The photograph was taken on 16th July 1949, soon after delivery, and conveys a typical high street scene of the period – the car following is a pre-war Singer 9.

From 1948 Guy Motors produced double-deck bodywork on Park Royal frames following an agreement between the two companies. The same year saw the options of a Wilson pre-selector gearbox, air brakes and a new 10.35-litre 6-cylinder diesel engine which had been developed jointly with Meadows for the Arab range. The Meadows option was not a success and the majority of customers stayed with Gardner engines. On the truck front, the Otter reappeared in 1948 with a stronger chassis frame and larger brakes with vacuum assistance.

During this period, companies in the motor industry were instructed by the Government to put exports first, much to the frustration of British motorists who very often could not purchase new models for some time after they were announced. At the same time, any vehicles imported from America had to be paid for in dollars.

As a result almost no new American vehicles were imported until some restrictions were lifted in the mid-50's. The shortage of trucks was partly resolved by the large numbers of ex-military vehicles, usually of British or American manufacture, which were being sold off from various sites around the country.

Britain was not alone in rebuilding its war-ravaged fleets and there was a great demand for new vehicles in many countries. Guy Motors did very well in the export markets in those early post-war years for apart from countries in the British Empire, the company built up an excellent reputation in Belgium and Holland. One order from Holland was for a batch of 120 single-deck Arab chassis which received very handsome Saunders bodywork.

In 1949 the company suplied some Arab chassis to Red & White Motor Services fited with a 5-speed Meadows constant mesh gear box.

Southampton Corporation followed its eleven pre-war and eight utility Arabs by 35 Mark II chassis with metal-framed bodywork to post-war style by Park Royal in 1946 and then a total of 150 Mark III, again with Park Royal bodywork, delivered between 1948 and 1953. Guy supplied Southampton's entire post-war need for new buses until 1955. All the Arab III buses, including No.106 (FCR 196) of March 1948 seen here, and the last 20 Arab II, had Gardner 6LW engines and the Guy constant-mesh gearbox. Vehicles of this type remained the most typical Southampton bus until the late 'sixties. The access hole for the 6LW's oil filler continued to be much nearer the radiator than with the 5LW – compare with the 5LW utility Arab II illustrated on page 58.

The largest home-market customer for the Arab III single-decker was the Northern General Transport Co Ltd, taking 134 examples with 5LW engine between 1947 and 1950. They took the concept of a shorter bonnet further than the standard 5LW version, having a specially modified front-end design with more upright steering column and the bulkhead moved forward to allow the Brush body to seat 38 passengers, much as on similarly modified AEC Regal chassis for this fleet in 1939. This example, 1256, seen in Leeds, had been pressed into service on the Newcastle-Liverpool express route the month after entering service in July 1949. NGT, never a Guy customer until wartime, also chose the Arab with 5LW engine for most of its post-war double-deck needs until 1956.

The Guy Arab did well in Africa. Part of a batch of ten longwheelbase Arab III with 5LW engines for J. N. Zarpas & Co Ltd of Lagos, Nigeria is seen with bodywork nearing completion at the premises of Park Royal Vehicles Ltd. There had been fourteen similar buses the previous year and further repeat orders followed at intervals.

Facing page: JWS 581 was 301 in the fleet of Edinburgh Corporation, when photographed on route 3 on 1st August 1954. Upon withdrawal from London Transport 60 Guy Arabs were acquired by Edinburgh. Although the utility bodies were considered to be life-expired after only seven to ten years, due to problems of metal corrosion and of rot and movement in the timber body framework, their Guy chassis and Gardner engines had many years of useful life left in them. At this time, Edinburgh was replacing its tram system and these chassis were acquired as the basis of new motor vehicles for tramway replacement. The semi full-fronted body was designed by Duple and built by them or Nudd Brothers and Lockyer. These handsome vehicles, with their concealed radiators, and attractive mouldings on the front panels were to serve Scotland's capital city until 1969.

Left: FVD 742 was H42 in the Central SMT fleet in Scotland. It was one of sixteen Arab IIIs ordered in 1951, being fitted with Guy 53-seat lowbridge bodywork on Park Royal frames. The polished radiator is surmounted by the famous cast-aluminium Guy American Indian Head, bearing the legend 'Feathers in our cap' on the head dress band.

Centre left: Seen in Colmore Row in May 1951, Birmingham City Transport 2562 (JOJ 562) was one of a hundred Arabs built in 1950-51 using the standard Birmingham-style bodywork of the period, which included a 'new look' tin-front concealed radiator, in the design of which Guy was involved. Eventually the city had 301 of these buses, whose design had resulted from a partnership between BCT and Guy Motors in 1949. They incorporated 6LW engines, fluid flywheels and preselctive gearboxes as specified by the operator. Highbridge 54-seat bodywork was locally built by Metropolitan-Cammell and incorporated cantilevered rear platforms in the style of the London RTs. Delivered between 1950 and 1953, the last were withdrawn in 1977 which says much for the original concept.

Below: A 13ft-wheelbase Vixen with factory built cab and cattle truck body built by Bowyer Bros of Congleton, now known as Boalloy and producing curtain-sided and van bodies. Weighing under 3 tons it could legally travel at 30 mph.

Power came from a Gardner 6LW engine coupled to a 4-speed Wilson pre-selector gear box via fluid flywheel.

The new design became the MkIV Arab and introduced a new bonnet and grille assembly which did not meet with universal approval as it restricted visibility and hindered maintenance. As a result Guy Motors re-introduced a traditional design in 1953 with a new style of bonnet and wings. Production of the MkIII Arab continued alongside the MkIV until mid-'53.

Further improvements to the Otter range of trucks came in the early 'fifties with the option of the Gardner 4LK engine in 1950, followed two years later by the additional option of the popular Perkins P6 engine. Initially the diesel engined Otter had a different cab understructure, due to the fact that the Gardner engine was bulkier than the Meadows petrol unit, and a more rounded cab which was built in the Guy Motors body shop was fitted. During 1952 this cab was fitted to all types of Otter trucks irrespective of engine type.

For a number of years engineers had looked at the possibility of alternative positions for the engine when designing heavy vehicles. By the 'fifties, the manufacturers of heavy British

Although many towns and cities had disposed of their tram systems in the 'twenties and 'thirties, others, such as Birmingham, did not replace their trams with buses until the 'fifties and 'sixties, often because there simply were not enough new buses available for the conversion. An order was received from Birmingham City Transport in 1950 for 100 Arab chassis. The chassis was a new design to comply with the authority's requirements and, amongst other changes, the rear platform was not self-supporting.

Above right: Recalling memories of past chivalry, the conductor helps passengers aboard Midland Red 3563 (MHA 63) whilst working Route 243 to Cradley Heath in August 1951. This BMMO classified type GD6 was a Guy Arab III with an attractive Guy body on Park Royal frames, new in 1949. Originally fitted with a Meadows engine, it was subsequently equipped with a BMMO engine.

Left: The Birmingham and Midland Motor Omnibus Company, or Midland Red as it was better known, designed and built much of its own fleet until the break up of the company under NBC. Vehicle number 2550 (HHA 2) was photographed loading well at Leicester St. Margarets in October 1950. It was one of a number of Guys drafted in during the difficult wartime years. Its Weymann utility body has been much rebuilt and restyled by Brush of Loughborough. Part of the somewhat ungainly frontal treatment has been improved by the chromium-plating of the radiator shell.

Below: At the 1952 Commercial Motor Show, the Perkins P4 diesel engine became available in the Wolf and Vixen chassis. An early delivery was this 10ft 7¾ wheelbase Wolf diesel van which went to a food manufacturer in 1953.

Above: A 14ft 9in wheelbase Otter diesel with a Gardner 4LK engine, coachbuilt cab and 16ft long dropside body, owned by a West Bromwich haulage contractor working under contract to carry Cerebos salt from Middlewich in Cheshire.

Below: Pictured on 18th August 1951 in an East Midland urban setting is No. 44 (DFW 169) in the fleet of South Notts of Gotham.

For many years Guy vehicles were popular in the Low Countries. This Arab III was one of 120 ordered by Guy's Dutch distributor in 1947. The handsome body is by Saunders and seated 45 passengers.

This August 1951 view shows L550 in the fleet of Red & White Services, in the company's smart red and cream livery. Seen in this broadside angle, the stylish lines of its Duple metal-framed lowbridge 53-seat body are accentuated. Platform doors were fitted to the rear entrance. It was one of 25 with Gardner 6LW engines dating from 1949-50.

Below: This handsome Arab III owned by Moores of Kelvedon in Essex is typical of the half-cab luxury motor coach of the late 1940s and early 1950s, which will fire many happy memories for older readers of days at the seaside. The driver reverses his coach on 15th July 1959, when it still looks in fine condition in its green livery. On the nearside pillar in front of the entrance door can be seen one of the old-style directional trafficator arms. Moores were eventually taken over by Eastern National in 1963, taking into stock their Guy fleet, including this vehicle, a 5LW engined model with Strachans coach body dating from 1949.

One of the first operators other than Birmingham City Transport to receive the Arab in Mark IV form, complete with 'new look' front, was the East Kent Road Car Co Ltd, which followed batches of Arab III double-deckers, the standard double-deck choice for the fleet since 1950, with 29 Arab IV in 1953, all with 6LW engines, GFN912 being shown here before delivery. They had Park Royal metal-framed four-bay bodywork built to a curvaceous style having some affinities with the London RT and which suited the new front-end very well.

Further along the south coast, Southdown Motor Services Ltd took a more conservative view though in this case favouring basically similar vehicles. Leyland had long been Southdown's standard make of chassis, but a big fleet of wartime Arab models had been followed by twelve Arab III in 1948 and then in 1955 another dozen were of Arab IV type with 6LW engines and Park Royal bodywork, of five-bay layout and slightly more 'upright' design. Here the traditional style of front was favoured, and this view of 515 (OUF 515) shows how radically altered the new model was in its proportions as well as many mechanical details, as compared to the Arab III. The radiator no longer projected forward and styling changes included a sloping bonnet top and front wings lacking the upturned leading edge. A further 36 generally similar buses followed in 1956.

single-deck bus chassis had opted for the underfloor engine. Probably the first really successful bus design in which the engine was moved from the front of the chassis was the revolutionary American Twin Coach of 1927. Designed by Frank and William Fageol, the design used two 55bhp 6-cylinder Waukesha petrol engines mounted under the seats behind the front axle, thus leaving the interior of the vehicle clear of any mechanical intrusion. In Britain during the 1930s there was the AEC Q and later in the decade the Leyland FEC for London Transport (LT type code TF) which had the distinction of being the first true underfloor design to go into service in Britain.

A few truck manufacturers also took up the idea of the underfloor engine. White offered a 12-cylinder petrol-engine of 9-litres in the impressive T730/731 range of 1935. Sentinel put a range of diesel engined underfloor trucks into production from 1945. Albion, Dennis and Commer also used the underfloor engine layout. Had it not been for the Second World War, the underfloor engined bus would undoubtedly have appeared a decade earlier.

Guy Motors introduced the Arab UF (underfloor) at the 1950 Motor Show. The successful mounting of the Gardner engine in a horizontal position resulted in Gardner later marketing the HLW range of engines. The conversion work on the LW engine was carried by Guy Motors and the handsome body offered by the factory again used Park Royal frame work.

One of the earliest customers for the new model was Huddersfield Joint Omnibus Committee, followed by Red & White Motor Services. The latter ordered fourteen chassis which were fitted with Duple Roadmaster bodies, a design immortalised by Dinky Toys in an age when anything other than a model London bus was a rarity.

Following on from the UF Model was LUF, introduced in 1952. The L stood for Light, a weight reduction being achieved by greater use of alloys. Home market customers bought the LUF whilst the heavier UF sold to overseas customers and both models continued in production until 1959.

Below: Huddersfield Joint Omnibus Committee's Arab UF No. 1 (FVH 1) stands beneath the trolleybus overhead on 24th March, 1952. The driver is climbing into his cab through the external swing door, which was still adhered to by some bodybuilders at the time, rather than obtaining entry through the saloon. Guy bodywork wears the Huddersfield red livery with cream and black lining. The transfer on the windscreen and nearside indicates one of the earliest uses of a full-size single-decker for PAYE service.

Foot: Lancashire United 518 (STF 203) is pictured in Lower Mosley Street, Manchester in June 1954, working the Tyne-Tees-Mersey service which was the normal preserve of these vehicles, soon after delivery. Its Weymann 40-seat bodywork has dual-purpose seats and is in red bus livery. Alongside is contemporary Yorkshire Traction 1002 (GHE 2) a Leyland Tiger Cub with Saro body.

The Otter chassis for 30-seat bodywork was re-designed in 1950 and the Gardner 4LK diesel engine was offered as an alternative to the Meadows petrol engine. The 4LK was not the most refined of diesel engines but it was beautifully made and long lasting. There was a need for 6-cylinder diesel and in 1952 the company offered an additional alternative to the 4-cylinder Gardner, which was the Perkins P6.

The Otter was similar to the Vixen apart from different sized wheels/tyres and a heavier chassis and components. London Transport ordered 84 Vixen chassis, fitted with the Perkins P6 engine. Now universally known as the GS class, the chassis were fitted with neatly styled bodies in the London Transport style of the period by Eastern Coach Works. The Guy model designation was NLLVDP. The frontal styling incorporated the bonnet and wings from Ford of Britain's ET range of trucks which had entered production on 2nd March 1948.

The Ford ET range used a Briggs cab which shared pressings with certain English Dodge models and the Leyland Comet. In addition to London Transport, Douglas Corporation later bought a variation of the NLLVDP/GS design, best remembered for the bodywork's excessively large destination boxes and known as Wolsley's Camels after the then General Manager of the undertaking.

The Otter truck was fitted with a new all-steel Motor Panels cab in 1953 and became the Otter MkII. At this time there was increasing competition in the 6/7-ton truck market. However, the real competion would come from Luton in the shape of the new 7-ton Bedford S type. Introduced at the 1950 Commercial Motor show, the new Bedford would soon justify Bedford's advertising slogan and you really did 'see them everywhere'.

In 1953 Guy Motors made a few Big Otter diesel trucks. Powered by a Gardner 4LW, the new design could legally carry a 7½-ton payload. Two years later another attempt was made to compete in this section of the truck market. A new fibreglass cab, based on a Motor Panels design but 6in wider, was produced at the Fallings Park works. By reducing the weight it was now possible to carry an 8-ton load. Power was initially by either a 68bhp Gardner 4LW or an 80bhp Meadows 4DC330; later Leyland's 100bhp O.350 and AEC engines were offered.

In 1954 a spectacular display at the Commercial Motor Show introduced the new heavy duty Goliath models, covering a gross weight range from 14 tons to 24 tons. The display consisted of an 8-wheeler, 6-wheeler and 4-wheeler mounted on one another, piggy-back fashion, with steps to enable the public to inspect all three vehicles. An AEC chassis was used for the new range, together with a cab which was also used at the time by ERF and BMC. In order to give the design some individuality, Guy Motors used their own front panel which incorporated a grille. A small enamelled Indian's head was fitted at the top of the name casting.

The rear panel of the Goliath incorporated a single central rear window and the end result was a neat and attractive design. Power units comprised the usual 5-and 6-cylinder diesel engines from Gardner in addition to the 6-cylinder 130bhp Meadows 6DC630. The name of the new range was changed to Invincible, as the name Goliath was used in export markets by the German company Goliath-Werke GmbH, which was part of the Carl FW Borgward group which collapsed in 1961.

Considering that Guy had been out of the 'heavy' market for some 20 years, the new range was reasonably successful, no doubt helped by the general high regard in which the company was held, and the components used.

Above: The original and early post-war Otters had the same cab as the Vixen. A new cab and understructure was designed for the diesel-engined version, but, in 1952, this was also fitted to the petrol-engined chassis. This example has an integral cab with a large kerb viewing window and sliding doors.

Below: Joint author Robin Hannay, in his younger days, standing in front of a Vixen recovery vehicle which had just been finished by the body shop. The chassis had been built from spares by the service department in 1953.

Above: The conductor with his Bell Punch ticket machine and cash bag awaits time, before setting off on route 12 to Sheffield in 1960. Over the paling fence can be spotted a Ford 5 cwt delivery van. Weymann 53-seat lowbridge bodywork of attractive styling is fitted – similar batches were found in the Midland General fleet and as London Transport's RLH class, albeit on AEC chassis. ONU 285 was number 185 in the smart green and cream fleet of Chesterfield Corporation. The Guy Indian proudly surmounts the radiator.

Below: Darlington Corporation had operated an exclusively singledeck trolleybus fleet, so when it was decided to replace them with buses the initial choice was Guy Arab III buses, using the a 30ft-long version of the single-deck 5LW-powered chassis, on which special centre-entrance 41-seat bodywork was built by Roe. No.33 (PHN 706) of the initial batch supplied in 1952 is seen here some years later, by which date double-deck Arab buses were also in service.

Above: The Duple Roadmaster body, well known from the contemporary Dinky Toy model, was built on Guy Arab UF and Leyland Royal Tiger chassis. One of the UF examples for Red & White Services Ltd of Chepstow is seen entering Victoria Coach Station, London, soon after entering service in 1952. By that date Red & White had been taken over by the British Transport Commission and was soon to be brought into line with Tilling Group practice, standardising on Bristol-ECW products and so the 14 Guys of this type remained unique in the Red & White fleet.

Below: Harper Brothers of Heath Hayes were operating this Burlingham bodied coach when it was photographed on 16th October, 1960. The chassis was a UF and the bulbous bodywork shows an early attempt to incorporate twin headlights in a design dating from the late 'fifties.

Above: The new range of heavy vehicles re-introduced an old name – the Goliath. This is an early 6LW powered example which was exported to East Africa, where the Guy name was already well known for the reliability of the Arab bus chassis.

Below: In the 1950s Guys had an excellent export business, most vehicles were sent CKD (completely knocked down) packed in large crates. To convey these to the docks, a Meadows 10-litre powered Invincible 8-wheeler was added to the works transport fleet in 1955 fitted with a Guy-built alloy platform body. In this case, however, the load was an Arab Mark IV single-decker destined for the China Motor Bus Company of Hong Kong.

Above: To meet the requirements of the Daily Mirror group for delivery of papers from the presses to the railway termini, Guy supplied a fleet of Wolf vans. They had Boalloy bodies which concealed the radiator. The 3.7-litre 58 bhp petrol engines fitted gave a lively performance. This is one of the first, delivered in 1955.

Below: This Norwich operator bought a lot of Guys in the 1950s. Powered by the 130 bhp Meadows 6DC630 engine with a 5-speed overdrive gearbox, the Invincible 8-wheeler had a 4,000 gallon tank.

Above: The Mk3 Otter entered production in 1957 and was similar to the Mk2 but featured a fibreglass grille over a block-type radiator and a 5-speed David Brown gearbox. This 1958 model has a 16ft-long cattle truck body mounted on a light platform body. As the container was removeable, it was not counted in the vehicle's weight, enabling it to avoid a 20 mph speed limit.

Below: A tractor unit was available in the Invincible range. This was an exhibit at the 1956 Commercial Motor Show in the colours of a Manchester operator, on the British Trailer Company's stand, also from Manchester. The trailer was of the '4 in line' type where each pairs of wheels were mounted on short axles fixed to a spring between them. This gave a higher-carrying capacity than the usual single axle.

Above: An 8-wheeled Invincible owned by R. H. Gibson & Co Ltd, a Cheshire haulier now renamed Compass Aggregates. The Edbro tipping gear was of the under-floor type favoured at this period and incorporated a stabiliser. A Gardner 6LW 112 bhp engine was fitted and a 16-ton payload could be carried in the Boalloy tipping body. The AEC origin of the chassis, axles and suspension is readily apparent in this view.

Below: At the request of British Road Services, Guy designed a tractor version of the Otter. Powered by a Perkins diesel engine with a 4-speed gearbox and two speed rear axle, it was intended for eight to ten ton payloads. Seen delivering a David Brown tractor, this vehicle was owned by Staffordshire Farmers Ltd of Wolverhampton.

Above: The Invincible chassis could be supplied without a cab, if required. H. G. Pentus Brown from Leighton Buzzard bought this Meadows-powered Invincible 8-wheeled chassis and had an alloy cab built by Homalloy of Preston in 1956.

Below: The brewery industry had traditionally needed a driver with two mates to unload the barrels and crates when delivering to pubs. To enable a wider 3-seater cab to be fitted, this Otter diesel had front wings normally used on the passenger version. Alloy bodywork kept the weight under three tons.

Above: The speed restriction on vehicles weighing over three tons still applied in the 1950s. This 14ft 9in wheelbase Otter diesel powered by a 4LK Gardner engine was fitted with an aluminium cab and body built by Homalloy of Preston, and weighed under three tons, allowing it to travel at 30 mph. It was photographed on its way to the 1956 Commercial Motor Show. The chassis and rear wings were covered in brown paper to prevent damage to the high gloss finish of the paintwork.

Below: A 13ft 9in wheelbase Warrior with the standard Meadows 4DC330 engine photographed outside the Guy drawing office in Park Lane, Fallings Park. A 17ft-long tipping body was fitted with 4ft-high fixed sides.

One of the leading Guy distributors was T. G. B. Motors Ltd of Burnley. They were also engineers and were known for their third axle conversions. This 1958 15ft 8in wheelbase 4-wheeler has had a second, steered front axle fitted by them, increasing the gvw by four tons and allowing an additional 3-ton payload.

After the purchase of the Sunbeam Trolleybus Co. in 1948, production of these vehicles continued in the Sunbeam factory until 1953, when production was transferred to Fallings Park where an extension had been built to the machine shop. Sunbeam's export models produced in the post-war years were very well received in overseas markets. Generally, the export models had a longer wheelbase. A good example was the MF2B model, built in 1950 for one-man-operation, with the entrance in front of the front axle whilst the exit could be either between the axles or behind the rear axle.

In 1954 the company received an order for 15 Sunbeam F4A 2-axle chassis from Walsall Corporation Transport Department. Their General Manager, Mr Edgley Cox, had obtained permission from the Ministry of Transport to operate 30ft-long double-decker trolleybuses on 2-axle chassis; at that time the limit for double-deck bodywork on a 2-axle chassis was 27ft. The chassis for Walsall were fitted with very striking Willowbrook bodies, providing seating for 68 passengers.

As a result of the success of this experiment, from 1st July 1956 the law was changed and the 2-axle 30ft double-decker became legal. Further trolleybus orders received

around this period included short wheelbase MF2B for Kingston-upon-Hull, which were used for one-man-operation. Bournemouth took 39 chassis between 1958 and 1962 and had the distinction of being the last home market operator to order trolleybuses.

With a world-wide demand for vehicles in the late 'forties and early 'fifties, some 60 per cent of Guy Motors production was going abroad and earning valuable currency for Britain. The company was very fortunate in having two brothers who made an ideal partnetship – Sydney Guy, a first-class engineer and Ewart Guy, a first-class sales director, the latter providing the sales expertise and the human touch which both brothers' attitude manifested itself in the company's personnel record.

The export drive had its moments, one being a problem which had manifested itself in some overseas countries, where it was discovered that the ash frames of some truck cabs made ideal meals for termites! This was one reason for the introduction of modern steel and fibreglass cabs.

Another problem which affected British manufacturers of cars, commercial vehicles and buses in this period was that many of their designs which performed satisfactorily on smooth British roads proved to be inadequate on dirt roads or continental pavé. The same had been true pre-war, but exports had not then formed such a high proportion of overall production. It was the reason why 70 per cent of the cost of a Packard went into the chassis, engine/transmission and suspension. Even so, the Packard body

was more robust than an equivalent quality British vehicle.

Another problem which was giving cause for concern at Guy Motors in the late 'forties and early 'fifties was the production of too many models from too great a range of components. It was hoped that the solution lay in using 'variations on a theme', with the minimum number of additional parts and by concentrating on the areas of the market that the mass producers did not cover. The result of this policy, which was put into action far too late, was the very successful Invincible II and Warrior II range which appeared at the Commercial Motor Show from 1958 onwards.

For many years Guy vehicles had been very popular in South Africa. The company's affairs were looked after very satisfactorily by agents appointed by the company to deal with all matters concerning sales and service. However, in 1955, Guy Motors decided to open their own outlets in South Africa and the decisions made by the board of

Quite a high proportion of wartime Arab buses had long careers, even though their original bodywork often suffered from rot of the wood framing due to the poor quality of timber then available. New bodies were built in many such cases, but Southdown carried out a thorough rebuild as well as making subtle improvements in appearance when modifying some to open-top for such services as that to Beachy Head. This Arab II was one of several with Park Royal bodywork so treated.

directors were ultimately to lead to ruin. By the end of the decade such large sums of money had been pumped into the venture that in 1959 the Guy Motors board was warned of the possible collapse of the company if it did not pull out of the South African enterprise. This advice was ignored with the inevitable and catastrophic collapse in 1961. But we anticipate our story, and the successes and failures which were just around the corner which we shall see in the following chapters.

P.R.V. GROUP BODY SALES DIVISION

ROE

Following the prototype all-metal body, ROE of Leeds have now been instructed to produce twenty-five "Wulfrunian" bodies for the West Riding Automobile Co. Ltd.

PARK ROYAL VEHICLES LTD, ABBEY ROAD. LONDON. N.W.IO.
TELEPHONE: ELGAR 6522

Facing page:
Production of trolleybuses in the Fallings Park factory spanned some three-and-a-half decades, beginning with the first local examples for Wolverhampton through to the splendid Walsall and Bournemouth Sunbeam vehicles of the 'fifties. Possibly the most remarkable survivor among early Guy trolleybuses, seen opposite, was one from the original fleet built in 1928 for Hastings Tramways. One of eight BTX models with open-top Dodson bodywork, it was retained after the rest of the type were replaced, and operated as a tourist attraction, as seen here. When Maidstone & District Motor Services Ltd, which owned the business from 1935, replaced the system with buses in 1959 this vehicle continued to be operated from time to time by the use of a Commer TS3 diesel engine, mounted in place of the electric motor.

The final trolleybuses for Walsall were particularly distinctive. They hold an important place in history as the first 30ft-long two-axle double-deckers to be allowed to operate in Britain. This was under special dispensation when they entered service in 1954 but their successful operation paved the way for general approval for both motor and trolleybuses of this configuration from 1956. Willowbrook built the bodywork to an unusual design with very broad corner pillars at the front of the upper-deck but curved-glass panels in the corresponding corner cab windows below. The resulting appearance was decidedly controversial as can be seen in this illustration of No. 870 operating an enthusiasts' tour.

Above: Charles H. Roe Ltd had been associated with Park Royal Vehicle Ltd since 1948 and by the late 'fifties often acted as PRV's 'special order' department. For Guy's advanced Wulfrunian bus chassis, a metal-framed body partly based on the Park Royal design developed for the rear-engined Leyland Atlantean was used. Among its special features was the nearside staircase which allowed more circulating space on the front entrance platform, inevitably cramped by the space needed for the front-mounted Gardner 6LX engine fitted as standard. As described in the next chapter, the Wulfrunian incorporated a remarkable combination of advanced features, notably air suspension and disc brakes neither of which had been successfully devdeloped for use on a double-deck bus at that date and indeed the Wulfrunian showed up the need for development capabilities far beyond the scope of a modest-sized manufacturer.

The Guy Motors stand at the 1958 Commercial Show must have impressed many of their customers. An exciting range of truck and bus chassis was on display for the first time, and the future looked very bright on the surface.

The Victory and the Wulfrunian, the two new bus chassis, together with the first 30ft Arab IV chassis were displayed on the company's stand. The Arab IV was fitted with a full front Burlingham body with forward entrance, for Wolverhampton. Over the next three years 50 more were placed in service by Wolverhampton Corporation. These new bus chassis, together with the new Invincible II, meant that Guy Motors had the most advanced range of vehicles at the 1958 Commercial Motor Show. The new heavy duty truck range drew high praise from all quarters, including the Minister of Transport. Many people consider, to this day, that these cabs were some of the best looking ever to grace a truck chassis.

The new Invicible II range consisted of four 4-wheel chassis, two twin steer six-wheel chassis, three ordinary six-wheel chassis and two eight-wheel chassis. Five makes of engine were offered, including Gardner's new 6LX which produced 150bhp, Rolls Royce C6 and Cummins HU, HF and NH. The most powerful of these, the Rolls

Royce C6, produced 210bhp. Other engines were the O.600 and O.680 from Leyland and the Meadows 6DC 500 and 6DC 630.

Gearboxes were by Meadows, Fuller, Leyland and David Brown. Amongst the many interesting features were split braking, air assisted hand brakes, curved windscreens, twin headlamps, two interior lights in the cab, comprehensive heating and demisting for the cab, plus a socket for an electric shaver and provision for an Ecko radio. The range was also available in normal control for the export market.

Commercial Motor summed it up when it referred to the styling being 'more like that of an American private car, yet without being too garish'. In the late 'fifties there were still a few pre-war heavies in every-day use. Any driver who turned up in a new Invincible in late 1958 or early 1959 would soon find his truck surrounded by admirers. For many, here was the truck of tomorrow.

By the mid-'fifties Guy Motors had become convinced that advances were needed in the ride-quality of buses and coaches, and that the answer lay with air suspension. General Motors had recently built coaches with air suspension for Greyhound in America who had had bought

Above: The Regent Oil Company bought a number of Invincible Mk2 eight-wheeled tankers. This example delivered in 1959 has a one-colour paint scheme which does not look as attractive as the livery it superseded shown on the adjoining vehicle. Note that the bumper bar has been fitted upside down.

Right: The Invincible Mk 2 6-wheeler was available with a short wheelbase for tipper work and two longer wheelbases for haulage use. This is the longest version fitted with a 24ft-long drop-sided body, and had partial Petroleum Regulation requirements fitted for carrying paint.

Lower right: Wynns of Newport ran general haulage vehicles in addition to their well-known heavy haulage outfits. This Gardner 6LX powered Mk 2 unit ran at 24 tons gross under Construction and Use Regulations.

Facing page:

Bulwark Transport being pleased with their Mk1 Invincibles placed an order for the new Gardner 6LX powered Mk 2 to be exhibited at the 1958 Commercial Motor Show. Thompson Bros (Bilston) Ltd built the 4000 gallon tank. Trevor Dvdley was the chassis designer of the new Invincible and Ron Thomas the stylist and cab designer. The exhibit for the Motor Show was driven to Earls Court by Raymond Baxter who gave a commentary for radio listeners on the way. The very advanced styling caused quite a stir at the show. Even 36 years after its introduction the Ron Thomas design still looks fresh. The chassis was now entirely of Guy design.

the GMC Type 4104 Scenicruiser, from mid-'53. The type 4104 rode extremely well, although it has been said that the roll on corners was considered excessive in Britain.

At this time many automotive engineers were looking at the feasability of air suspension on vehicles. Although General Motors had successfully engineered a system for the GMC type 4104 coach chassis, success was to elude them when a similar system was introduced on their prestige Cadillac Eldorado Brougham in 1957. At $13,074 the hand-built Eldorado Brougham represented the best of General Motors engineering yet despite the corporation's vast resources there were intractable prolems with air leaks around the domed air chambers. The majority of owners had the air system replaced by steel springs.

Guy Motors decided to develop its own air suspension and, encouraged by the West Riding Automobile Company who promised an order for 100 double-decker chassis if a suitable design were offered, the company came up with the Wulfrunian a chassis. The new chassis was an extraordinary tour-de-force for a company which by this time had limited financial resources. The Wulfrunian and Victory offered air suspension, disc brakes and independent front suspension.

The Guy Victory was aimed at the export market. The air suspension system was offered as an option but the air/hydraulic disc brakes were standard. A Leyland 150bhp UE680 diesel engine of 11.1-litres was coupled to a 4- or 5-speed Guy built semi-automatic gearbox via a fluid flywheel. Another advanced feature of the time was the fitment of an exhaust brake and examples of the chassis were sold to customers in Belgium and Holland. Being suitable for a 40ft body it was in its day a very advanced design.

Very little has been written concerning the Victory's reliability. Being lighter than the Wulfrunian, with better cooling available for the brake discs and generally used for long distance work, it would appear that it did not suffer as badly in terms of reliability as the Wulfrunian.

Unfortunately the Wulfrunian was another story. Many people had never heard of a Wulfrunian – a native of the town of Wolverhampton – and before long many more would wish they too had never heard the name.

Guy Motors had consulted with customers in the bus industry, seeking their ideas and requirements for a new low-height double-deck chassis. In addition a study was made of low-height chassis then in production. As a result of these studies the engineers and designers concluded that what was needed was a front-engined chassis 30ft long and 8ft wide which could seat 78 passengers. The chief engineer of the West Riding Automobile Company provided Guy Motors with useful information from the bus company point of view and his company became the main operator of the controversial Wulfrunian design, taking 126 of the 137 built.

The designers placed the engine alongside the driver at the front of the chassis. Five engines were offered with outputs ranging from the Gardner 6LW 112bhp to Leyland's O.680 of 150bhp. Other engines included Gardner 6LX, Leyland O.600 and AEC AV590. Two alternative gearboxes were listed, either a Guy-built semi-automatic unit or a ZF 4-speed syncro-mesh, with the option of 5- or 6-speed versions if required. The drive was taken to a dropped centre rear axle. The lobes for the air suspension unit were manufactured by Firestone, who had been involved with air suspension designs in America.

The front suspension of the Wulfrunian consisted of parallel wishbones of different

Above: The second and third Wulfrunian chassis received Roe bodywork of the type standard for the model and were delivered in 1960 as demonstrators, painted in the yellow and black livery derived from Wolverhampton Wanderers football colours. They had Gardner 6LX engines of 10.45-litre capacity as fitted to all but two of the model. The Cave-Browne-Cave heating and ventilating system, originally devloped on one of Southampton's Guy Arab III buses, was standard, with intakes each side of the destination box, but an indication of the engine position, offset towards the driver so as to give maximum platform space, is given by the louvres in the front panel.

Left and facing page: A brochure produced in December 1957 for the overseas Guy Victory model. Designed to take bodies up to 40ft long its most interesting feature was air suspension and when introduced in 1958 it was the first British bus to have air suspension on both axles. A Leyland UE680 150 bhp engine was standard, coupled to a 4 or 5-speed semi-automatic gearbox.

GUY Victory

DOMINANT FEATURES

- 6-CYLINDER SHORT-STROKE DIESEL FOR HIGH PERFORMANCE WITH LONG LIFE AND ECONOMY.

- LOW FLAT-TOP CHASSIS AVAILABLE WITH OUTRIGGERS FOR SEMI INTEGRAL BODY-WORK.

- CHOICE OF CONSTANT MESH, SYNCHRO-MESH OR EPICYCLIC GEARBOXES, 5-SPEEDS WITH OVERDRIVE OR DIRECT TOP RATIO.

- BENDIX-WESTINGHOUSE DUAL AIR PRESSURE SYSTEM TO 2-LEADING SHOE BRAKES—FOR EXTRA SAFETY.

- LONG PROGRESSIVE SPRINGS FOR FIRST CLASS COMFORT AND ROAD-HOLDING.

- HYDRAULIC OPERATION FOR CLUTCH AND ACCELERATOR FOR SMOOTH AND EASY CONTROL.

- MAXIMUM PERMISSIBLE GROSS WEIGHT:
  13 TONS (13¼ Kgs.)
  FRONT AXLE : 5½ TONS (588 Kgs.)
  REAR AXLE : 8 TONS (813 Kgs.)

8 LITRE DIESEL ENGINE — MEADOWS 6HDC500

The six cylinder horizontal engine is unequalled for power in the 8 litre class. Fitted below frame level in the Guy Victory, it has a maximum gross output of 161 b.h.p., and maximum torque of 346 lb. ft. at 1400 rpm. A direct injection system and special automatic advance governor ensure maximum fuel economy and instant starting from cold. "Square" bore and stroke dimensions give smooth running, low piston speed and low wear.

ENGINE DATA

Number of cylinders	6
Bore	120 mm (4.724 in.)
Stroke	120 mm (4.724 in.)
Capacity	8.14 c.c. (497 cu. in.)
Compression ratio	16 : 1
Max B.H.P. S.A.E. (gross)	161 at 2500 r.p.m.
Max B.H.P. (cont.)	150 at 2500 r.p.m.
Max torque	346 lb. ft. at 1400 rpm.
Piston speed	1980 ft. min. at 2500 rpm.
Overall height of engine	26 in. (660 mm.)
Overall width of engine	41 in. (1041 mm.)
Overall length (engine only)	51½ in. (1314 mm.)
Weight with flywheel and compressor	1740 lbs. (790 kgs.)

ENGINE SPECIFICATION

CRANKCASE AND BLOCK. Monobloc iron casting. Centrifugally cast, wet liners.

CYLINDER HEADS. Three detachable units. Removable valve seat inserts, centrifugally cast at high aluminium iron alloy. Stellite faced exhaust valves.

PISTONS. Die-cast light alloy with 3 compression and 2 scraper rings, one above and one below the fully floating gudgeon pin. Top compression ring chromium plated.

CRANKSHAFT. Oil hardened alloy steel, carried in seven 3.35 in. (85 mm.) diameter, pre-finished, thin shell, steel backed main bearings, copper-lead and lead-indium faced. Torsional vibration damper at forward end of crankshaft.

CONNECTING RODS. "H" section alloy steel forgings, designed to permit easy withdrawal through cylinder bores. Big end bearings are 3 in. (76 mm.) diameter and are the same type as the main, small end bushes are copper-lead fined steel, pressure-lubricated via oil holes in the con-rods.

CAMSHAFT AND VALVE GEAR. Supported in seven 2¼ in. (57 mm.) diameter, white metal lined bearings, pressure lubricated. Valves operated by cast iron bucket-type tappets through short pushrods.

AUTOMATIC ADVANCE. Fuel injection timing is automatically controlled by centrifugal governor between fixing gears and fuel pump, eliminating adjustments and routine maintenance.

INJECTION. CAV type injection pump base mounted on top of crankcase.

LUBRICATION. Forced feed to main and camshaft bearings, rockers and gear drives, supplied by gear driven pump in sump. Oil is drawn from the system approx. 4 gallon (18 litres) sump through a floating suction filter. Full flow canister type delivery filter has spring loaded by-pass valve. Scavenger pump draws and returns oil from pressure to sump.

In unit with the engine, the 5-speed box is available with constant or synchro-mesh gears and overdrive or direct top ratio. The rear engine mounting consists of a tubular cross member located through a bonded rubber bush in the bell housing.

Strength and accuracy in weight is ensured by a rectangular ground steel casing for the speed level screws, wheel and pinion and fully floating axle shafts. Progressive spring loan 13 main leaves with a rebound leaf and 3 overliners.

Generously dimensioned 2-leading shoe brakes are actuated by Bendix-Westinghouse direct acting diaphragm chambers with dual air pressure system. Good resistance to fade breaking torque is provided by the 1 section front axle beam.

CHASSIS DIMENSIONS

A	Overall length	35′ 6″	10833 mm.
B	Wheel base	18′ 0″	5486 mm.
C	Front overhang	7′ 0″	2133 mm.
D	Rear overhang	10′ 6″	3200 mm.
E	Frame height — front	2′ 11″	889 mm.
F	Front track — ground	6′ 7¾″	2020 mm.
G	Frame width	3′ 7¾″	1115 mm.
H	Frame width — rear	2′ 10″	863 mm.
J	Rear track	5′ 11½″	1814 mm.
K	Width over rear tyres	7′ 10½″	2425 mm.
	Width over outriggers	8′ 0″	2438 mm.

Above: The Warrior Light 8 had an AEC AV470 engine, 6-speed overdrive gearbox and 2-speed driving axle with a trailing rear axle as standard, giving it a good performance at 24 tons gross (then maximum for an 8-wheeler) and an extremely good payload, being about a ton lighter than most of its competitors. A Gardner 6LW was offered at a later stage.

Below: The Warrior was available as a tractor for operation at 22 tons gross train weight with a spiral bevel axle or 24 tons with the Eaton 2 speed. This was one of a fleet bought by Mobilgas but operated at 20 tons gross with a single axle trailer.

GUY Victory

DOMINANT FEATURES

- 6-CYLINDER SHORT-STROKE DIESEL FOR HIGH PERFORMANCE WITH LONG LIFE AND ECONOMY.

- LOW FLAT-TOP CHASSIS AVAILABLE WITH OUTRIGGERS FOR SEMI INTEGRAL BODY-WORK.

- CHOICE OF CONSTANT MESH, SYNCHRO-MESH OR EPICYCLIC GEARBOXES. 5-SPEEDS WITH OVERDRIVE OR DIRECT TOP RATIO.

- BENDIX-WESTINGHOUSE DUAL AIR PRESSURE SYSTEM TO 2-LEADING SHOE BRAKES—FOR EXTRA SAFETY.

- LONG PROGRESSIVE SPRINGS FOR FIRST CLASS COMFORT AND ROAD-HOLDING.

- HYDRAULIC OPERATION FOR CLUTCH AND ACCELERATOR FOR SMOOTH AND EASY CONTROL.

- MAXIMUM PERMISSIBLE GROSS WEIGHT : 11½ TONS (1376 Kgs.). FRONT AXLE : 5½ TONS (5588 Kgs.). REAR AXLE : 8 TONS (8128 Kgs.).

8 LITRE DIESEL ENGINE – MEADOWS 6HDC500

The six cylinder horizontal engine is unequalled for power in the 8 litre class. Fitted below frame level in the Guy Victory, it has a maximum gross output of 161 bhp. at 2500 rpm. and maximum torque of 346 lb. ft. at 1400 rpm. A direct injection system and special automatic advance governor ensure maximum fuel economy and instant starting from cold. "Square" bore and stroke dimensions give smooth running, low piston speed and low wear.

ENGINE DATA

Number of cylinders	6
Bore	120 mm (4.724 in.)
Stroke	120 mm (4.724 in.)
Capacity	8145 c.c. (497 cu. in.)
Compression ratio	16 : 1
Max. B.H.P. S.A.E. (gross)	161 at 2500 r.p.m.
Max. B.H.P. (nett)	150 at 2500 r.p.m.

Max. torque	346 lb. ft. at 1400 rpm.
Piston speed	1996 ft. min. at 2400 r.p.m.
Overall height of engine	36 in. (960 mm.)
Overall width of engine	41 in. (1041 mm.)
Weight with flywheel and compressor	1240 lbs. (769 Kgs.)

ENGINE SPECIFICATION

CRANKCASE AND BLOCK. Monobloc iron casting. Centrifugally cast, wet liners.

CYLINDER HEADS. Three detachable units. Replaceable valve seat inserts, centrifugally cast at high chromium iron alloy. Stellited and hardened inlet valves.

PISTONS. Die-cast light alloy with 1 compression and 2 scraper rings, one above and one below the fully floating gudgeon pin. Top compression ring, chromium plated.

CRANKSHAFT. Oil hardened, alloy steel, carried in seven 3.35 in. (85 mm.) diameter, pre-finished, thin shell, steel backed main bearings, copper-lead lined and lead-indium treated. Torsional vibration damper at forward end of crankshaft.

CONNECTING RODS. 'H' section alloy steel forgings, machined to within 1 oz. (28 mm.) diameter and are the same type as the mains : small end bushes are copper-lead steel, precision-lubricated : oil holes in the con-rods.

CAMSHAFT AND VALVE GEAR. Supported in seven 2¼ in. (57 mm.) diameter, white metal lined bearings, pressure lubricated. Valves operated by cast iron bucket-type tappets through short pushrods.

AUTOMATIC ADVANCE. Fuel injection timing is automatically controlled by centrifugal governor between fitting gears and fuel pump, eliminating adjustment and routine maintenance.

INJECTION. C.A.V. type injector pump base mounted on top of crankcase.

LUBRICATION. Forced feed to main and camshaft bearings, rockers and gear drives, supplies by gear driven pump, mounted in sump. Oil is drawn from its approx. power in sump oil case. Oil is drawn from its approx. A gallon (18 litres) sump through a floating section filter. Non-adjustable relief valve, diesel out-side filters case. Full flow canister type delivery filter has strong footed by-pass valve. Scavenger pump draws and strains oil from gearcase to sump.

Constructionally dimensioned 2-leading shoe brakes are actuated by Bendix-Westinghouse direct acting diaphragm chambers with dual pressure system. Good resistance to full braking torque is provided by the 'I' section front axle beam.

In unit with the engine, the 5-speed line is available with constant or synchro-mesh gears and direct or overdrive top ratio. The rear engine mounting consists of a tubular cross member located through a bonded rubber bushes in the bell housing.

Strength and economy in weight is ensured by a rectangular pressed steel casing for the spiral bevel crown wheel and pinion and fully floating axle shafts. Progressive springs have 13 mm leaves with a rebound leaf and 3 positions.

CHASSIS DIMENSIONS

A	Overall length	33' 6"	10211 mm.
B	Wheel base	18' 0"	5486 mm.
C	Front overhang	7' 0"	2133 mm.
D	Rear overhang	10' 6"	3200 mm.
E	Frame height — laden	2' 11"	889 mm.
F	Front track — ground	6' 7½"	2020 mm.
G	Frame track — ground	6' 3"	1910 mm.
H	Frame width — rear	2' 10"	863 mm.
I	Rear track	5' 11½"	1816 mm.
J	Width over rear tyres	7' 10¼"	2413 mm.
K	Width over outriggers	8' 0"	2438 mm.

Above: The Warrior Light 8 had an AEC AV470 engine, 6-speed overdrive gearbox and 2-speed driving axle with a trailing rear axle as standard, giving it a good performance at 24 tons gross (then maximum for an 8-wheeler) and an extremely good payload, being about a ton lighter than most of its competitors. A Gardner 6LW was offered at a later stage.

Below: The Warrior was available as a tractor for operation at 22 tons gross train weight with a spiral bevel axle or 24 tons with the Eaton 2 speed. This was one of a fleet bought by Mobilgas but operated at 20 tons gross with a single axle trailer.

Above: An early Warrior Light 6 owned by
Chas B Pugh is seen at the Guy factory.
Powered by a Leyland 375 engine, it had a
trailing rear axle. With an unladen weight of
6 tons 16 cwts, a payload of 13 tons was
carried. The calibrated 20 cubic yard tipping
body had an underfloor tipping gear.

Below: The cab for the Mk2 Warrior and Invincible ranges pioneered several new
features. The most noticeable one was the angular appearance, which was
followed by other manufacturers. The steel understructure and fibreglass cab was
built in Guy's own bodyshop. It was the first commercial vehicle to feature twin
headlights and had a heater as a standard fitment as was a sun visor. This is a
Warrior with a 1900 gallon tank that was built by the Steel Barrel Co Ltd of
Uxbridge, Middlesex.

Top left: A later version of the Warrior with the revised grille and bumper bar. Vehicles at this time used in connection with the motor trade for deliveries could be used on general trade plates, saving an amount of vehicle excise duty. By the time this picture was taken, Guy was a Jaguar subsidiary, the cars appropriately being Mark X saloons.

Centre left: The final version of the Otter Diesel had a fibreglass cab based on the Warrior/Invincible design which did not suit the chassis. The 4LK Gardner was the only engine available. This Luton van was operated by the Silentnight Co. of Barnoldswick in Lancashire.

Lower left: The collection of milk was controlled by the Milk Marketing Board who, whilst having a large fleet of its own tankers, also paid hauliers to collect milk in certain areas. This Warrior Light 6 was one of a few 6-wheelers in the country to be used for this purpose in the 1960s.

Following page upper:
Towards the end of production of the Warrior and Invincible range, a modified cab became available on both models, which was a foretaste of the Big J cab. The new cab had larger and deeper doors with semi-circular wing apertures. These opened to give access to steps in front of the wheel making access much easier. This Warrior Light 6 powered by an AEC AV470 engine was new in 1965.

Following page lower:
The longest wheelbase available was a 15ft 9in which allowed a 20ft-long body to be fitted although about two feet would have been lost with the fitment of the crane on this example delivered to an Essex firm in 1965.

An 18ft 2in wheelbase Warrior chassis was produced for PSV work, but a few received van bodies. This example, owned by a Hampstead, London operator carried mattresses from a manufacturer in Tipton, Staffordshire for deliveries in the London area.

lengths. The design allowed 6ins. of movement in the vertical plane with an alteration in track of only 3/8in. The suspension units were mounted over the kingpins in order to improve stability and resistance to roll. At the rear, the axle sat in a subframe and was located by rods attached to the top of the differential housing, with a Y-shaped member attached to the centre. Twin shock-absorbers were used, one either side of the axle. Four rolling diaphragm units, interconnected by a hollow beam, were incorporated at the rear. The suspension units were operated by air pressure which was controlled by levelling valves. These valves allowed air to enter the system when the suspension was compressed under load and expelled it when the load was released. In order to increase stability on S-bends Guy Motors patented a design with two levelling valves at the rear and a valve at each one of the two front units. The system gave a remarkably smooth ride when operating correctly. Four wheel disc brakes were a revolutionary feature at the time, when even the majority of motor cars were still fitted with drum brakes. The application of four wheel disc brakes to a bus chassis was another first for Guy Motors. The design had been deveoped by Girling initially for Guy Motors.

In February of 1961 Wolverhampton Corporation purchased the first of two Wulfrunians. The initial vehicle was fitted with an East Lancs front-entrance body. This was followed by an order for a modified Wulfrunian which was shown on the Guy Motors stand at the Commercial Motor Show of 1962. The entrance was placed behind the front wheels; the wheelbase was lengthened and the front suspension moved forward. Drum brakes replaced the disc system. The engine was a Gardner 6LX coupled to a 4-speed fully automatic gearbox.

The Wulfrunian soon earned a dreadful reputation and the last Wulfrunians were sold to West Riding in 1963, other operators very wisely chose the Arab V which was available from 1962.

Whilst on paper the Wulfrunian was at least twenty years ahead of its time, in every day service it was a disaster, not only for the operators who had bought the vehicles in many cases because of the proven ability of the company's Arab range, but for Guy Motors, for whom it was to prove one of the final nails in the coffin.

The new Invincible range established Guy as one of the leading manufacturers of heavy trucks. There were problems with the cab in later years when it was found by operators that the cab base rusted quickly. There were also instances of windscreens held in by stainless steel clips to prevent them falling out. The top half of the cab was fibreglass and the quality of finish varied according to when, between 1958 and 1966/7, it was produced.

The chassis design was first class and, with the best of the engine transmission variations offered, the result was a very good vehicle for the period.

With the arrival of the new decade, Guy introduced the Warrior II range. Available in three- and four-axle versions and known as the Warrior Light 6 and Light 8, the range was claimed to offer the largest payload on the lightest chassis in the vehicle's weight class and at the lowest prices. The three- and four-axle variants were joined by a two-axle chassis version. The Warrior tractor unit was popular with major distribution companies. The company's literature of the time showed vehicles in the livery of Tate & Lyle, the sugar refiners, and Mobilgas fuel. The Light 8 could carry almost a ton more payload than the Invincible or other current eight-wheel chassis.

After the success of the 1958 Show, with the Invincible range proving very popular, and the Warrior soon to be launched the casual observer would have thought Guy was in a better position than it had been for some years. Unfortunately this was not so and the combination of the ill-advised South African situation already mentioned, and a disastrous new model – the Wulfrunian – conspired to brings matters to a dramatic conclusion. Whilst these final pieces of the jig saw were being put into place another significant event was taking place not very far away.

Sir William Lyons would be the next major player in the Guy story. Like Sydney Guy he had built up his empire from nothing, starting in 1922 when two motor cycles set up a sidecar manufacturing factory in Blackpool, the Swallow Sidecar Company. Now, 40 years later his quality motor cars were known throughout the world for value for money and he was looking for further expansion.

Following page upper: Number 100 (UCX 276) in the fleet of County Motors of Lepton was one of a pair of Wulfrunians, built to the same specification as those for West Riding. It was pictured on 12th May 1992 in cream and blue livery. Bodywork was by Charles H. Roe and seated 43 on the upper deck and 32 on the lower with a front entrance. Cave-Brown-Cave heating was fitted and there was an illuminated offside advertisement panel. Because of the position of the engine along the nearside of the driving cab, the driver gained access through a swing door on the offside. After only a year in service 100 passed to West Riding, becoming fleet number 996. It was disposed of in January 1970 for scrap.

Following page lower: Wolverhampton were persuaded to buy only two Wulfrunians despite their local manufacturee. Number 71 (4071 JW) was the second of the pair and featured a centrally-mounted engine and a forward entrance behind the front axle, and front staircase. East Lancs bodywork was fitted seating 40 upstairs and 31 downstairs with an unalden weight of 9 tons. A sliding offside cab door was fitted. This was the sole example built with cam-operated drum brakes activated by an air-hydraulic system. It was in service for 10½ years being new in December 1962, withdrawn in May 1973 and scrapped by Sykes of Barnsley in August 1973.

Below: Photographed on 7th October 1961 soon after delivery is Accrington Corporation's No. 156 (35 VTF). This and sister vehicle 157 (36 VTF) were a pair of Guy Wulfrunians fitted with Gardner 6LW rather than the more usual larger 6LX engines. Because of the lack of front entrance on these particular buses, the engine was mounted centrally in the frames behind the radiator grille. These were the only two buses fitted with ZF 4-speed synchromesh gearboxes, rather than the more usual semi-automatic type. 66-seat, rear entrance open platform bodywork by East Lancs was carried. Number 156 entered service in September 1961 and was withdrawn in January 1968, being sold to Ronsway Coaches of Hemel Hempstead. Sadly the same mechanical and suspension problems plagued these vehicles throughout their lives. By August 1971 both No. 156 and No. 157 had been broken up.

See previous page for captions.

Above: The MCW Orion was one of the least attractive double-deck bodies available and gained nothing in a vain attempt to produce a more modern-looking fully-fronted bus. Local operator Wolverhampton Corporation bought 30 Guy Arab Vs from Fallings Park in 1961. MCW bodywork was 30ft long and had a front entrance. Had the radiator grille and radiator filler been incorporated into a more aesthetically pleasing style, which reflected the windscreen line, a more attractive design might have resulted. Wolverhampton 54 (4054 JW) was photographed on 19th April 1969.

Below: On route 71 to Bolton on 17th August 1968, Lancashire United 234 (WTE 157D) demonstrates the 30ft Arab V chassis and 6-cylinder Gardner diesel. Front-entrance bodywork is by Northern Counties and seats 73. As was customary by that time, the radiator is concealed. Lancashire United was a major Arab user, with 88 of the final Arab V type with its slightly lower frame.

Guys position by early 1960 was not one of which the company would have been proud. It was only three years or so since the Founder had retired but the company finances were now in a perilous state, to the extent that Guy was trading whilst virtually insolvent. With a good product range, apart from the Wulfrunian, and a loyal and dedicated workforce the company was ripe for a takeover. Donald Stokes from Leyland had already been to look round but declined to make an offer.

William Lyons might also have declined at this time, but events were to take a different course. On 26th May 1960 the Jaguar company announced that it was to double in size. At the time the Government of the day was very keen to encourage motor manufacturers to set up new factories in areas of high unemployment. The system failed because the politicians did not take into account the considerable additional expenses any manufacturer would incur in transportation costs between sites. Lyons was a very astute business man and realised that the only way

forward for Jaguar cars was to stay as close as possible to the Brown's Lane site in Coventry. On 18th June in the same year Jaguar purchased the Daimler company and its factory, which was literally only a few miles from the Jaguar site, from the BSA group for £3,400,000.

Daimler's history goes back to 1893, when F. R. Simms formed the Daimler Motor Syndicate to exploit Gottlieb Daimler's motor vehicle patents. The first British Daimler cars appeared in 1897 and over the ensuing years the company became a major competitor to Rolls Royce in the luxury car market, in addition to becoming one of Britain's leading manufacturers of buses and coaches.

Continued on page 110

For the 1962 Commercial Motor Show Boalloy produced this special cab on a Gardner 6LX powered Invincible Mk3 tractor unit for a large Scottish operator. It is seen prior to collections by Guys. A chromium plated bumper bar remained to be fitted.

Above: The 15ft 9½in wheelbase Big J6 qualified for operation at 22 tons gross in the UK. Delivered in 1966, this Gardner 6LX powered example had a drop sided tipping body for carrying just of 14 tons of sand. Genefax Transport was the haulage subsidiary of General Refractories of Sheffield.

Below: Seen being loaded with scrap, the 1966 Big J4T owned by Renwick Haulage of Exeter is pulling a tandem axle tipping semi-trailer operating at 32 tons gross.

Above: This 1966 Big J8 had a Cummins V6 170 bhp engine and an 18ft-long steel tipping body fitted on a 14ft 9in wheelbase chassis, and was used by a Kent operator on civil engineering work.

Below: Boalloy of Congleton's main output in the 1950s and early 1960s was alloy tipping bodies. This 22ft-long example with fixed sides and Edbro twin ram tipping body was used for carrying sand from the Northwich area of Cheshire.

Right: Blue Circle Cement ran a large fleet of Big J8s. This 16ft 10in wheelbase chassis has a 24ft-long alloy platform body and deep valances at the side to enhance the vehicle's appearance. Both rear axles were driven.

Below: Castrol, the lubricant specialist, was a good customer for various types of Guy models from the 1950s to the 1970s. This J4T tractor unit was new in 1978 and had a Rolls Royce 'Eagle' engine.

Foot: British Road Services had been a regular customer of Guys for many years and bought large numbers of Big J4 tractors. Operated by their Oldbury (Birmingham) depot, this 1968 example has been fitted with a bolster on the fifth wheel coupling to which this steel girder has been attached by chains, whilst a tandem axle bogie was fitted at the rear.

Above: This 1977 Gardner 6LXCT, 240 bhp powered Big J4T was the last of a large number of Guy lorries that have been owned by this firm situated on the Cheshire/ Staffordshire border, and gave thirteen years excellent service.

Facing page upper: Another well-known operator from Wednesbury had bought Invincible tractor units and continued when the Big J was introduced, Coopers specialised in traffic to and from Scotland where they had another depot in Blantyre.

Facing page lower: The Big J4 was introduced at the 1964 Commercial Motor Show. It used a steel cab built by Motor Panels of Coventry, who also supplied them to other manufacturers. This 12ft-wheelbase chassis has Telehoist Loadlugger skip-handling equipment.

Left: R. Hampton & Sons were based in Moxley near Wednesbury in the West Midlands. They built up a large fleet of Big J4Ts. This 1970 model is seen loading sheet metal at their main customers, The Patent Shaft and Axletree Company in Wednesbury – a 200 year-old company that becacme a victim of the recession in the 1980s.

This Big J4T entered the well-known Scottish fleet of Sam Anderson in 1967 who had depots in Glasgow, Manchester, Birmingham and London, and specialised in carrying steel.

For several years Wincanton Transport ran a large number of Guy Big J4Ts. This one is pulling an insulated tank semi-trailer.

A Big J6 haulage chassis powered by a Rolls Royce 'Eagle' 220 bhp engine, new in 1975. It has a sleeper cab and the rear-mounted crane was used for lifting machinery. Owned by Hanlon and Wright of Stalybridge, Greater Manchester, it was withdrawn in 1990.

The 'Q' prefix gives no clue to the age of this AV505-engined Big J6, or its history. Built in 1973 as a stock chassis, it was subsequently fitted with a Simon elevating platform and sold to the Copenhagen Municipal Authority. However, as it did not conform to Danish vehicle regulations, it could only run within the city limits and was restricted to 20 mph. It came back to the UK in 1987 and was bought by Rhoburt of Poynton, Cheshire who are lighting contractors. It was due for replacement in 1992.

One of two recovery vehicles placed in service by Kennings in 1966, these Big J6 chassis have 220 bhp Cummins engines coupled to AEC 6-speed gearboxes. This example is still in use in 1994.

Originating with a Staffordshire operator, this Big J8 with Gardner 6LX engine was new in 1967. Seen in later years working for a Fairground operator, it featured a separate engine and radiator behind the cab as a generating set.

The Daimler company was also well-known as a manufacturer of military vehicles and during the early years of the 20th century produced a quality range of trucks.

Jaguar's timing in purchasing Daimler could not have been better. Daimler was about to launch the Fleetline rear engined bus chassis which in a few years became the most popular model in its class on the market.

The following year the South African losses, together with escalating warranty costs on the Wulfrunian, brought Guy to the point of no return and a receiver was appointed. In the last few years of independent operation Guy Motors had been losing £300,000 a year, despite the success of the Warrior and Invincible models. Sadly there could be no going back and the astute Lyons expanded again when Jaguar purchased Guy Motors for £800,000 in October 1961.

At his first meeting with the Guy directors, William Lyons informed them that their salaries would be reduced and pension rights stopped. The directors were told that there was no money but that they would be expected to pull the company out of the mess it had got into. Some directors were told that their services were no longer required.

Jaguar took a long look at the situation and decided that they would have to rationalise the range. Almost immediately, production of the 7-ton Otter truck ceased. Further cutting back took place and other models in the Invincible range were discontinued.

On the other hand the strength of the marque and its loyal following was not overlooked. Lyons recognised that there was little point in trying to compete with Bedford and Ford in the medium weight sector and so Guy's efforts would be concentrated in certain niches in the heavy end of the market. As part of that policy the following year saw the launching of the Mk III tractor unit at the Commercial Motor Show.

Facing page upper: Under apartheid, Africans often lived in townships a long way from their work and were transported by bus or rail with weekly or monthly tickets subsidised by the government. Putco Ltd, an Italian-owned company built up a fleet of 3,000 buses and the Leyland name disguises one of many Guy Victory Big Js running services out of Johannesburg where it is seen. These services ran for the most part over good tarred roads but the high floor level was retained in the interests of standardisation.

Facing page lower: The Guy 3-axle 'Megadeckers' were acquired by Johannesburg Municipal Transport in the late 1950s mainly for peak hour duties on routes where wiring for trolleybuses could not be justified. The 3-axle chassis, bodied by Bus Bodies South Africa, was specially produced for the South African market but the front end, known as the Johannesburg front, enjoyed brief popularity in the UK and was fitted to some models including the Chester example seen on page 117.

Below: *Commercial Motor* published this list of models, with specifications and prices, when the Jaguar rationalisation plan was announced at the 1962 Commercial Motor Show. The passenger vehicle range comprised the Wulfrunian and Arab Mk V double-deckers and the Victory J export single-decker.

STANDARD GUY GOODS MODELS FOR 1963

Model	Wheel-base		Gross weight	Engine	Gearbox	Rear axle	Old price inc. cab	New price inc. cab
	ft	in	tons				£	£
Warrior Light-4	8	9	20	A.E.C. AV470		single-speed	2,705	2,468
	or							
	9	0		Leyland O.400			2,515	2,346
"	"	"	"	Gardner 5LW		two-speed	2,890	2,750
"	10	6	14	A.E.C. AV470		single-speed	2,770	2,478
"	"	"	"	Leyland O.400		"	2,580	2,356
"	"	"	"	Gardner 5LW		"	-	2,665
"	13	9	"	A.E.C. AV470		"	2,770	2,488
"	"	"	"	Leyland O.400		"	2,580	2,366
"	"	"	"	Gardner 5LW		"	-	2,675
"	15	9	"	A.E.C. AV470		"	2,770	2,498
"	"	"	"	Leyland O.400	Six-	"	2,580	2,376
"	"	"	"	Gardner 5LW	speed	"	-	2,685
"	18	2	"	A.E.C. AV470	constant	"	2,790	2,508
"	"	"	"	Leyland O.400	mesh	"	2,610	2,386
"	"	"	"	Gardner 5LW	gearbox	"	-	2,695
Warrior Light-6	15	3	20	A.E.C. AV470	standard	"	3,310	2,905
"	"	"		Leyland O.400	equip-	"	-	2,769
"	17	9	20	A.E.C. AV470	ment	"	3,310	2,915
"	"	"	"	Leyland O.400	on all	"	-	2,779
Warrior Light-8	15	3	24	A.E.C. AV470	models	two-speed	3,610	3,385
"	"	"	"	Gardner 6LW		"	-	3,750
"	17	9	"	A.E.C. AV470		"	3,610	3,395
"	"	"	"	Gardner 6LW		"	-	3,760
Invincible 4-whlr.	8	9	24	Gardner 6LX		{single-drive} {double-red'tion}	3,470	3,330
"	17	9	14	Gardner 6LW		"	3,575	3,100
Invincible 6-whlr.	11	0	20	Gardner 6LX		"	4,035	3,875
"	13	9	20	"		"	4,035	3,885
"	17	9	20	"		"	4,035	3,895
Invincible 8-whlr.	17	9	24	"		"	4,335	4,130
"	15	3	24	"		"	4,335	4,120

Above: This Johannesburg street scene shows one of the Guy 3-axle Megadeckers in its later years after having been rebuilt with front entrance and the rear platform enclosed for one-man-operation. The vehicles seated 85 passengers with room for 20 standees, were 34ft long and 8ft 6in wide and were powered by Rolls Royce 12.17-litre diesel engines. The Megadeckers were amongst the world's largest double-deckers at that time.

Below: The BET-controlled United Transport Group was one of the largest users of Guy Big Js in Africa, large numbers being acquired for service in east, central and south Africa. These three Gardner-powered examples were part of the 300-strong fleet of the Vaal Transport Corporation, operating over very indifferent roads in the Southern Transvaal and Orange Free State and were photographed for a comparison of experimental liveries.

Amongst the improvements in this new model the overall height of the chassis frame was reduced. The vehicle offered a proven power line with a Gardner 6LX engine providing the power, which was fed through a David Brown 657 gearbox. The wheelbase of the tractor unit was 8ft 6in.

Further expansion of Jaguar's empire occurred in 1963 when the well-known fork lift truck, firepump and grand prix racing car engine manufacturer, Coventry Climax, was purchased. This was followed a year later with the acquisition of Guy's next door neighbour, Henry Meadows, the engine and gearbox manufacturer. Within a remarkably short space of time, through Lyons perception, Jaguar had acquired some of the best British companies in their respective fields. Had the Jaguar group remained independent it could have offered a product range to compete with the best in the world.

In 1964 Guy's final truck range arrived. The Big J (Big Jaguar) models were designed by Cliff Elliott. William Lyons had persuaded Elliott to leave Dodge Trucks where he had been responsible for the highly successful range of models that Chrysler's British truck factory produced throughout the 1950s and the aim was to introduce a Daimler truck. With the purchase of Guy, Cliff Elliott moved from Daimler to Fallings Park and the end result was the Guy 'Big J'.

Shown to the public for the first time at the 1964 Motor Show, the new design featured a Motor Panels cab which was also used by Seddon, Scammell and Foden. Following on from the Warrior II range, the chassis was available in 2, 3, and 4-axle variations. As with the Warrior, the cab entrance was forward of the front axle. A wide range of engines and gearboxes was offered, with a choice of AEC AV470 (later 471 and 505) and Leyland 401, as well as units from Cummins, Gardner and Rolls Royce. ENV gearboxes were used with the smaller capacity engines and AEC 6 or 12-speed splitters in the heavier models. The AEC gearboxes were later superseded by Fuller units.

The Big J range also replaced the Invincible range. A policy of progressive improvement was followed by the factory with the Big J range resulting in a reliable and competitively-priced truck which was popular at home and in overseas markets.

William Lyons was a very shrewd business man but in 1966 what might be seen with the benefit of hindsight as an error of judgement on his part led to the eventual downfall of Guy Motors and, almost, the downfall of Jaguar.

In 1965 Jaguar had made a record profit of £1.6 million net and 25,963 cars had left the Brown's Lane plant. The Big J range was proving extremely successful, as was the Daimler Fleetline bus. The XJ6 was only three years away, a car that would show the world the engineering talent behind the Jaguar name. Throughout the previous years a number of large motor manufacturers had come to Brown's Lane showing an interest in Jaguar; one of these was Leyland.

William Lyons was 64 years old in that year and it is likely that he considered that the best long-term future for his company was as part of a large group but remaining autonomous. He chose the British Motor Corporation, best known for Austin and Morris cars, with whom a deal was made in 1966, setting up the short-lived British Motor Holdings combining BMC with the Jaguar group. He obtained much needed funds to put the XJ6 into production but had tied his company to an ailing giant, and he was not to know that it in turn would merge with the Leyland Motor Corporation to form the ill-fated British Leyland Motor Corporation. The decision which Lyons took thus led ultimately to Guy becoming part of Leyland, an organisation which was effectively killing off competition by the purchase – and closure – of the opposition. So it would be with Guy.

As part of the expanding Jaguar organisation since 1961, the products of Fallings Park had been well received in the market place. In particular the Big J was gaining an excellent reputation as a robust vehicle which offered very good value for money.

On 11th July 1966, a joint statement was issued by Sir William Lyons, chairman of Jaguar, and George Harriman, chairman of the British Motor Corporation, stating that the two organisations were to merge to form British Motor Holdings. There were those in the trade who felt that in taking such a step Sir William had made the wrong decision and later events were to prove them right. However, such judgement nowadays has the benefit of hindsight and at the time there seemed to be impressive arguments in favour.

BMC was formed in 1952 when the Austin Motor Company and the Nuffield Group (Morris) joined forces. Of the two companies, Austin was the stronger, with two factories, the main works at Longbridge, Birmingham and the Vanden Plas works at Kingsbury to the north of London. The Morris empire, which had since 1940 been known as the Nuffield Group, comprised sixteen plants, though its main factory was at Cowley, Oxford.

The late Laurence Pomeroy Jnr said of the two companies that "Austin and Morris had made their reputation by the construction of sound reliable cars designed by successive generations of engineers who must have had a common sympathy with the sentiment expressed by the Duke of Cambridge: 'All change at any time and for any purpose is utterly to be deprecated'." But that was changing.

The Jaguar group, in addition to its highly successful cars, had taken up commercial vehicle manufacture with enthusiasm, initially inspired by Sir William Lyons' immediate and very shrewd realisation of the potential of the Daimler Fleetline double-decker and then of Guy, the latter seen more especially as a maker of goods vehicles. But Sir William saw a need for expansion, notably to be able to invest adequate sums in the forthcoming XJ6 car.

In 1966, BMC appeared to be a highly successful concern riding high on the innovative reputation built up since 1959 of the Mini, 1100 and 1800 models, all based on Alec Issigonis' concept of front-wheel-drive using a transverse engine position to produce compact yet internally roomy cars with handling characteristics far better than their competitors – and indeed their layout has been widely copied throughout the world. Not so obvious at that stage was the poor development, causing reliability problems and more seriously the undermining of the whole enterprise by the disastrous labour relations, with frequent strikes. Japanese competition was yet to have any significant impact in Britain, but the seeds of major trouble were there beneath the surface.

Superficially, the BMC-Jaguar merger was tidy, in that the two constituents' ranges barely overlapped, with BMC as the mass-producer and maker of lighter types of commercial vehicles and Jaguar the specialist car maker and, through Daimler and Guy, manufacturer of heavy-duty highly-quality buses and trucks. Thus was British Motor Holdings born, with high hopes.

As with other British vehicle manufacturers, BMC's costing was often poor, which meant profits suffered. Because of patchy quality control and poor design at Austin and Morris, by 1968 the new organisation British Motor Holdings had ceased to make a profit.

Leyland had begun to build up its empire on commercial vehicles, starting in 1951 with Albion Motors Ltd of Glasgow and followed in 1955 by Scammell Lorries Ltd of Watford. The group had also begun to become interested in cars, beginning with the take-over of Standard-Triumph, based in Coventry in 1961. This firm had proved to need much management attention, and indeed its acquisition is now seen as a first fateful step towards disaster. Leyland put Stanley Markland in charge. He was a direct-speaking Lancastrian who was a first-class engineer and had been the director in charge of Leyland's factories. His absence from Leyland was to be missed but at Coventry he pushed the Triumph 2000 into production and this was probably the best product of the Coventry factory under Leyland ownership. Improvements in quality helped to turn matters round.

Meanwhile the Leyland Motor Corporation, as it became, grew through further acquisitions, including that in 1962 of the Associated Commercial Vehicles Group, most notably AEC but also Park Royal (with a long history of co-operation with Guy). More car involvement came with Leyland's take-over of Rover in 1966.

This was a time of intense merger-fever, much of it encouraged by the Labour Government, which saw it as a solution to the growing financial problems of some of the major car makers. Yet some of the mergers created difficult situations. The Pressed Steel company made bodies for several major car makers and its acquisition by BMC in 1965 had placed Rover in a difficult position and the implications would not have been lost on Sir William Lyons. A decade earlier Jowett had to cease production when its body supplier, Briggs, was bought by Ford. There was talk of the Rootes group – making Hillman, Humber and Sunbeam cars and Commer trucks – and already with a shareholding by the American concern, Chrysler, becoming linked to Leyland, with Government encouragement.

Although those talks came to nothing, the Labour Government of Harold Wilson encouraged the merging of BMH and Leyland. In February 1967 Anthony Wedgwood Benn, nowadays better known as Tony Benn, who was Minister of Technology, made a statement in the Commons informing the House that BMH and Leyland were holding

Above: Gross vehicle weights were increased again in the 1960s, the short 3-axled chassis going up to 20 tons gross, but the Big J6 was designed for 22 tons gvw for export. This 11ft-wheelbase AEC AV505-powered chassis had a double drive rear bogie and was used as a demonstrator by the concrete mixer manufacturer.

Below: Built in 1968 this Gardner 6LX powered Big J8 van was purchased by a well-known Wolverhampton paint manufacturer. Two sliding doors were fitted on the nearside to assist unloading.

"BIG J"

GREAT NEW HEAVY DUTY RANGE FROM GUY

A striking piece of Guy advertising showing the new Big J, with Jaguar's Series 1 E-type alongside, subtely conveying the link between the two through common engineering excellence.

preliminary discussions. In October 1967 Leyland made an outright bid for BMH. The announcement was made public on 17th January 1968. The new company was to be the fifth largest of its kind in the world.

A few weeks later, on 14th May, the British Leyland Motor Corporation formally came into being. Leyland had begun to put its stamp on the car subsidiaries it had already acquired.

Whilst those merger negotiations were proceeding sales of Guy bus and coach chassis for the home market were dropping considerably, although demand from overseas was still buoyant.

A bus variant of the Warrior truck chassis had been designed at very short notice in 1958 for a Greek customer. Fitted with a vertically mounted Gardner engine, the design evolved into the Warrior Trambus. This name, which appears to have Dutch origins, was applied to single-deckers with the entrance ahead of the front axle, usually with the engine also mounted at the front alongside the driver.

By 1965 the Warrior Trambus had been replaced by a new version of the Victory chassis which was based on the Big J truck chassis and was available with an AEC AV505 engine. The Victory Trambus later became British Leyland's heavy duty export bus chassis. It replaced the AEC Ranger, Albion Clydesdale and the Leyland Worldmaster.

In 1969 the final batch of Arab V chassis were delivered to Chester Corporation. The production of Guy bus chassis for the British market finished with this order. The introduction of the Bus Grant, a government scheme designed to encourage operators in modernising their bus fleets through the availability of a grant towards the cost of new vehicles, initially 25% and later increased to 50% of total cost, was ironically to prove the means by which many of the most reliable British bus chassis would become outdated. The grant depended upon the vehicle complying to a specification which had been designed to ensure that only vehicles suitable for one-man-operation would qualify. Thus the rear-engined Atlantean/Fleetline/VRT suddenly had a clear advantage over models which many operators would have preferred to continue to purchase such as the Arab V, Regent V, or Leyland Titan. Leyland discontinued all three models. Ironically, the Wulfrunian would have fitted the specification without any problem having been designed with front entrance and being suitable for one-man-operation. Unfortunately its unreliability had killed it off before it could have become a contender.

In South Africa, operators had discovered the disadvantages of early British rear-engined double-deck bus chassis. Whilst the ease of entry was appreciated by passengers, maintenance departments soon encountered reliability problems. Although the Victory J or Trambus chassis had been designed for single-deck bodywork the City Tramways Group asked Bus Bodies SA Ltd to modify a Victory J chassis to take double-deck bodywork. The end result was extremely successful leading to a further order for chassis from Guy Motors. Considerable work had to be done to reduce the floor height; however, remarkably, there were only six components which were not common to the standard single-deck chassis. An initial batch of 80

was built, starting in February 1973 and by July 1975 the total in service had reached 103. A Mk II version was designed, in which the front axle was moved further forward with the entrance/exit immediately behind the front wheels. In all, 152 Mk IIs were produced.

Due to the success of these vehicles, an order was received in South Africa for four Mk Is for the Kowloon Motor Bus Company of Hong Kong.

Leyland had intended to close Guy Motors in the mid-'seventies but the success of the Big J range, well-suited to markets where rugged design counted for more than sophistication, forced them to keep the factory open.

In 1975 the first of the Landtrain T43 models appeared, a vehicle which is remembered for being featured in the Yorkie Bar TV advertisement. Production of the T43 continued at Wolverhampton until the factory closed, when it was transferred to Bathgate.

During the final years of production some Leyland Marathon trucks, were assembled at Fallings Park. It was an attempt by Leyland to compete in the premium truck market against the new opposition, from Volvo and Scania in particular, but only a small budget was allowed for its development.

In 1978 an improved single-deck Victory Mk II was shown for the first time. The suspension was designed to cope with off-highway operation and the braking system now incorporated a 'hold' facility so that the bus could be held at stops without exhausting the air brake reservoir. In addition to the single-deck chassis, a double-deck chassis was also shown. This became known as the Victory II Series II.

The new double-deck chassis was derived from the CRT type Leyland Worldmaster and incorporated the layout and running units of the Victory II chassis. British Leyland was forced to put the new design into production or risk losing a highly valued customer, which had already placed an order with Dennis for their very similar Jubilant chassis. Production of both chassis continued at Guy Motors until 1982. With the closure of the Guy Plant in that year, production of the Victory chassis moved to the newly renamed Farington Bus Plant, leaving the new Leyland Assembly Plant to concentrate solely on trucks.

Almost to the end of production the Guy plant was recruiting new staff. Some were taken on, only to be dismissed a few weeks later. Guy's last display was at the NEC, Birmingham for the 1980 Commercial Motor Show. Many orders were taken but quite a few of these vehicles were not built at Wolverhampton. Nearly 800 Victory chassis were made up at the Farington plant between 1983 and 1986 almost all of them being exported in CKD (completely knocked down) form for assembly overseas. The Victory had proved a remarkably successful model and 2,115 had been produced at both Fallings Park and Farington in the period between 1981 and 1986.

Why was Guy Motors closed? By the late 'seventies Leyland was losing sales to the opposition. The once proud name of Leyland, now unfortunately and irrevocably tarnished through the car association, had become the butt of jokes and the name was now associated with poor quality and unreliability. The new truck assembly plant, laid out in accordance with modern thought and having excellent facilities, was too big for Leyland's requirements

118

alone. Doug Jack, a former Leyland sales manager, in his book *Leyland Bus – The Twilight Years*, recalls that when the Leyland Assembly Plant was opened it was big enough to handle the output of all the British truck manufacturers – and that was before the recession.

The T45 range, which was the group's big hope for the 'eighties, was late in getting into production. It was a well-designed range and began to restore Leyland's name as a premier truck maker as the new models came into production though it has to be said that it did not compare favourably against the best of the continentals.

The Guy factory was old and needed modernising, as did some of the plant, but the workforce was second to none and could still custom-build a vehicle to an operator's requirements in a remarkably short space of time. This was one of the great attributes of a craftsman based factory.

Another problem was the Leyland attitude. There was the assumption, often put across with considerable arrogance, that the Leyland way was the only way. Interviews with retired employees from all factories closed by Leyland bring out this unfortunate fact, confirming that there was a feeling at Leyland that no-one else could possibly know anything which might be of value to Leyland.

To make matters worse this situation often existed in factories such as Guys where full order books and profits should have ensured that the value of the company would be recognised – more especially when Leyland itself was running into deep trouble.

Whilst it is true to say that eventually common sense prevailed, and a more enlightened attitude improved relations between Lancashire and the various satellites, the initial damage which this arrogance had created was never to be forgotten and soured many people's perception of the Leyland organisation.

The closing of Guy, Bristol and Scammell, all of which produced products of the highest quality, leads one to believe that the Leyland policy of so-called rationalisation was in fact a pretext for removing competition. In fairness it must be recorded that over-capacity within Leyland and the industry in general meant that some factories would, inevitably, have to close. What is hard to swallow for those who lost their jobs as a result of this situation was the fact that many of their employers were still profitable when the workforces were put out to grass. In later years Leyland was to close its various bodybuilding plants in an attempt to safeguard the Lancashire, and later Cumbrian, manufacturing facility and the same bitterness was engendered time and again.

The closing of Guy Motors is considered by many to be an act of criminal folly which is remembered to this day in Wolverhampton. Whether Guy might have survived without the Leyland involvement can only be conjecture but certainly its forced marriage with Leyland was the kiss of death. As an ex-member of the management team said recently, every time he sees a Hino truck he thinks to himself. "Guy could have made those, and exported them in large numbers."

How then shall we remember Guy ? An organisation with a skilled and respected workforce producing quality products for a discerning market, and, at the end, operating profitably. In common with many other manufacturers it was working in an outdated factory but if a fraction of the money which had been ploughed into one part of Leyland's bus empire could have been made available for modernisation at Fallings Park that problem could easily have been resolved. A proposal had been mooted in 1979 to inject £175 million into Leyland's Scottish plants but no such plans were proposed for Guy.

In 1982 Guy was closed when it had a full order book for eighteen months ahead and was the only BL plant other than Land Rover to make a profit.

So much for Leyland's rationalisation !

Facing page upper: The last of a batch of seven, Chester Corporation 30 (330 YFM) waits amid the characteristic half-timbered buildings of this old city, before performing on route 9 to Pipers Ash. Powered by a 6LW engine, the chassis is a 30ft Arab IV, on which is mounted a front entrance 73-seat body by Massey Bros of Wigan. The front grille and bonnet assembly are in the 'Johannesburg' style and it is interesting to see a large destination box above the entrance. It entered service in 1962. Chester was to have the honour of taking the very last Arab.

Facing page lower: Lancashire United was a classic example of a loyal Guy supporter which became 'converted' through the wartime utilities. Before the war the company had been purchasing Dennis and Leyland models, with only two Guy motor buses joining the fleet and clearly not impressing the engineering department. Some sixty Utility Arabs made a very different impression and LUT subsequently bought Guys until 1968 when there were no more to be had. This splendid Arab V, dating from 1965 now resides in the Museum of Transport in Manchester as a lasting memorial to the marque.

119

Individually built

FOR LONGEST LIFE AND LOWEST RUNNING COSTS

Individually built really means something—mass production in its generally accepted sense is not practised at Guys. Every vehicle is built by skilled craftsmen and the greatest care is taken in fitting and inspection at all stages.

A Guy vehicle will run economically year after year with a minimum of attention and will maintain this performance for a long working life. Mass-produced vehicles cannot be expected to have this extra stamina and will prove a less sound investment in the long run.

FITTED BOLTS ARE USED THROUGHOUT THE CONSTRUCTION OF THE FRAME AND MEMBERS WITH THEIR OBVIOUS ADVANTAGES OVER RIVETS.

Like all proud companies Guy was not slow to promote its image. There were those who would have commented, with justifiable feeling perhaps, that individuality is all right but having common components which are fully interchangeable is also a desirable aim. Guy were not always known for the latter! Author Broatch, currently involved in the restoration of a 1966 Warrior Light 6, and knowing a thing or two about other Guys, feels entitled to pass this remark whilst confirming that he still thinks that Guys are great machines with loads of character.

One of the oldest preserved Guy vehicles is this 1935-built Guy-bodied splendid former Llandudno UDC Wolf with bus bodywork. It is seen here being prepared for a Trans-Pennine run, and the radiator with the original Guy logo incorporated will be noted.

Below: A pair of smart Park Royal-bodied Arabs – a wartime example from London Transport on the left and an Arab III from East Kent on the right. The Southampton vehicle at the foot of the page illustrates the wartime anti-blast and blackout measures applied in connection with the D-Day commemorations in 1994 though the vehicle in question is a post-war model.

Below: Swindon Corporation was one of the first fleets to receive an allocation of Utility buses and this Weymann-bodied example is seen taking a break at Harry Ramsden's famous chip shop en route to Harrogate on yet another Trans-Pennine run from Manchester.

Left: The post-war Guy radiator with the Indian's head was a handsome design which will always be remembered with affection.

Right: A 1948-built Arab with Crossley bodywork operated by Blackburn Corporation. It now resides in the St. Helens Museum of Transport awaiting major bodywork attention.

Right centre: Southampton Corporation built up a large fleet of Park Royal-bodied Arabs in the post-war years and this example has been retained as a working museum piece.

Below right: Birkenhead Corporation was another staunch supporter of the Guy marque and No. 242, a wartime Arab II is seen here on the famous Madeira Drive at Brighton at the end of a London to Brighton HCVS run. It carries Massey bodywork, in this case built in 1953.

Below: Chester Corporation became one of the last operators to run Arabs and this Massey-bodied example, No. 1, is retained by the operator. It is seen in Heaton Park, Manchester on a Trans-Lancs run.

Right: Edinburgh Corporation operated this 1948-built Arab. The Metro-Cammel bodywork demonstrates the 'Scottish' rear entrance incorporating a cutaway – as standard on all double-deck open-platform vehicles to allow passengers to escape in the unlikely event of a vehicle turning over onto its nearside. Edinburgh was another user which became attached to Guys following experience of the wartime models.

Centre right: Guy built the 35-seat rear-entrance bodywork and the chassis for this former Central SMT single-decker, now restored in Western livery and representing similar vehicles operated in the Kilmarnock fleet. It bears close affinity to contemporary Burlingham designs, though perhaps neater in outline. The ex-York Pullman double-decker in the background indicates that this photograph was taken on another preserved vehicle run.

Below: Half-canopy Guy single-deck coaches were never particularly common but this smart Roe-bodied Lancashire United example is a regular attendee at rallies and is always splendidly turned out. It was one of ten purchased in 1951 and had 37-seat bodywork. In typical LUT tradition the batch could be found working excursions, private hire, workman's services and school services whilst buses operated the longer distance services.

One of the best-known preserved Guy vehicles is Geoff Lumb's Waveney-bodied Wolf which for many years took holidaymakers around the Great Orme in Llandudno. It has probably done even more miles since it was acquired for preservation, being a regular attender – and cup winner – at a large number of rallies each season for many years.

Upper centre left: This Wolf was one of two operated by the Guy service department, which received registrations GUY4 and 5. The bodywork was built by Guy and the vehicles were used for delivering spares and attending roadside breakdowns.

Lower centre left: This Vixen 4-ton drop-sided lorry had just emerged from the Guy bodyshop when it was photographed by apprentice Robin Hannay in the early 'fifties.

Below: Tony and Brian Niblett own this 1950 Wolf with Ormac 20-seat bodywork. It operated with MacConnacher of Ballahulish for over thirty years until purchased for restoration. It is seen at the Birmingham outer-circle run in 1994.

Foot of page: Ron Lucas, Chairman of the Guy Owners Club, provided this photographic opportunity with his Otter diesel lorry, left, and Wadham-bodied Vixen coach right. The three vehicles were posed at a Birmingham rally.

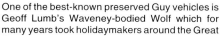

Southampton extended the lives of some of its late 'forties-built Arabs by converting them to open-top and repainting them in a predominantly cream livery as shown. This example was photographed on a private hire working from Waterlooville to the Southsea Spectacular vintage vehicle rally .

Edinburgh Corporation demonstrated good Scottish thrift by its purchase of 60 former London Transport wartime Guy Arabs. These were rebodied by Duple and exhibited an unusual feature whereby the nearside window aperature of the full-fronted body was not glazed — was this further thrift ? It was actually to allow easier access for maintenance, of course. Presumably the mechanical bus-washer had not then arrived in Edinburgh.

This Lincoln Corporation Guy Arab Mk III now in the care of the Lincolnshire Vintage Vehicle Preservation Society carries Guy bodywork, incorporating Park Royal framing. There is a suggestion that the close association between Sydney Guy and Bill Black, both of whom were involved in wartime utility bus development, led to Guy using PRV frames for its double-deckers and underfloor-engined single-deckers. The cowling replacing the radiator hides a Ruston air-cooled diesel engine built locally in Lincoln. The conversion is remembered by conductors, who claim they were unable to hear passengers speak, and drivers who could hear nothing at all above the roar of the engine.

Above and right: Guy worked closely with Birmingham City Transport in the design and development of a new double-deck bus chassis of which 300 were ultimately ordered. This example has recently been fully restored after eleven years hard work. The specially-produced coat of arms with Guy logo sits well on the 'tin front' design on which Birmingham was to standardise. The Arab Mk IV was a development of this chassis for other operators.

Below and centre right: London Transport also produced an attractive emblem on its Guy Special models, these being bodied by Eastern Coach Works of Lowestoft. Close examination of the various Indian's heads reveals that London Transport"s Indian is of leaner build and has had his eyes opened. Cause and effect ?

A high proportion of Llandudno UDC's fleet ended up in the hands of preservationists. Whilst the fleet has become Aberconwy, many of the vehicles are still around. Amongst the last to be purchased were two Roe-bodied Otters with Gardner 4LK engines. This one was photographed in Manchester's Heaton Park during the Trans-Lancs rally in 1994. The sunshine belies the fact that the vehicle was just about to become bogged down in the waterlogged grass.

Above: Bournemouth was always known for the quality and finish of its fleet, especially its trolleybuses. In 1962 it purchased its final batch of electric vehicles, Sunbeam MF2Bs built in the Guy works at Fallings Park and fitted with Weymann dual-door bodywork. They were destined to have only a short life for before the end of the decade the Bournemouth trolleybus system would be no more. Notice the difference in the volume of road traffic in this picture when compared to modern day Bournemouth.

Ronald Edgley Cox earned himself the reputation of an individualist, and the vehicles operated in his fleet reflected his sometimes unusual pioneering spirit. It must be said, however, that his 30ft-long 2-axle trolleybuses paved the way for an easing of the regulations affecting double-decker buses and trolleybuses in the UK. The Willowbrook body was of somewhat unusual outline as can be seen but the vehicles performed well in service giving fast and comfortable riding qualities to the citizens of Walsall and, occasionally, Wolverhampton. Some of the latter would no doubt have been involved in the construction of the chassis at Fallings Park.

The final years of bus chassis manufacture saw Guy producing the Mk IV Arab and the Wulfrunian. The latter was ahead of its time in design but was doomed to failure due to lack of development, leading to the introduction of the very successful Arab V which was to be Guy's UK swansong. Many operators would mourn its passing, for its rugged simplicity and reliability were key features in any fleet. The rear-entrance Northern Counties-bodied Lancashire United model, above left, is another example of a fleet remaining true to Guy almost to the end of production, following experience with the wartime Arabs. The Wulfrunian, seen above right, will always be associated with West Riding who instigated the design and clearly lived to regret it. Of the 143 built some three or four survived into preservation, but only this one is now complete.

Chester Corporation had the honour of taking the final batch of Guy chassis built for the home market and these Arab Vs were delivered in two batches, each of three, during 1969. The first of the six is seen here with its forward-entrance Northern Counties bodywork in the distinctive Chester livery. Number 47 remains in the Chester fleet, performing special duties from time to time, and gave some twenty years' reliable service. It seems safe to say that had the model continued in production Chester would have continued to purchase it – unfortunately the Bus Grant was to put a stop to Guy bus chassis production for the home market.

1914	30 cwt Model J
1920	15 cwt JA
1920	V8 car
1920	2/2½ ton chassis
1920	3 ton BB chassis with 'Spud' wheels
1921	4-cylinder 12 hp and 15.9 hp car model G
1921	JA 1 tonner
1922	O Model 30 cwt chassis
1923	4-cylinder 13/26 car model H (last Guy car)
1923	Guy 30 cwt Articulated
1923	Guy 2/3 ton battery electric
1923	Road Rail Vehicle
1924	Vehicles for War Office including Half Track
1925	BX 5 tonner
1926	BAX and FBAX (both rear axles driven for military)
1926	ON
1927	CAK 7 tonner
1927	FCAK 7 tonner (Forward Control)
1927	Gas Producer truck
1927	Star flyer (coach chassis)
1929	Star Planet & Comet (car)
1930	FC6 Warrior 4-wheeler 6 ton payload
1930	Goliath 6-wheeler 10 ton payload
1933	Wolf 2/3 tonner – Vixen 3/4 ton
1935	Fox (6-wheel Otter)
1935	Otter 6 tonner
1941	Vix-Ant
1947	Wolf & Vixen reintroduced
1950	Otter 6 tonner
1953	Big Otter Diesel 7½ tonner
1953	Otter Mk II
1954	Goliath/Invincible 14 to 24 ton
1955	Big Otter renamed Warrior
1957	Formidable tractor unit
1958	Invincible II range
1960	Warrior II range
1962	Invincible III tractor unit and forward step cab
1964	Big J range (last Guy design)
1975	Landtrain (produced spasmodically until factory closed in 1982)

Also from mid 'seventies onward Scammell Crusader
was assembled spasmodically

GUY TROLLEYBUSES 1926-1949

Year	Model	Control	Wheels	W/B	Seats	SD or DD
1926	BT32	Forward	4	173½	32	SD
to	BT48	Forward	4	163½	54	DD
1949	BTX60	Forward	6	-	60	SD&DD
	BTX66	Forward	6	-	66	DD

The last 'all-Guy' trolleybuses were sold in the period 1947-49. These were 70BTX double-deck and 50 BT double-deck. Following the purchase of Sunbeam in late 1948 all trolleybuses were marketed as Sunbeam.

GUY/SUNBEAM TROLLEYBUSES 1949-1962

Year	Model	Control	Wheels	WB	Seats	DD or SD
1949-54	F4	Forward	4	-	62	DD
1949-62	MF2B	Forward	6	-	70	SD or DD
1954-62	F4A	Forward	4	-	70	DD

GUY BUS AND TROLLEYBUS

Year	Model	Control	Wheels	W/B ft in	Seats	SD or DD
1914 to approx 1925	J 30 cwt	N/C	4		16-20	SD

(Note some vehicles quoted as 1 ton chassis around 1920 also from 1923 small wheels were available, these models known as Runabout.

Year	Model	Control	Wheels	W/B ft in	Seats	SD or DD
1924	BA	NC	4	13 4	20	SD
1924	B	NC	4	15 3	25	SD
1924	BB	NC	4	16 5	25	SD
1925	BK	NC	4	16 5	25	SD
	(Premier Six)					
1926	FBB	Forward	4	16 5	35	SD
1926	BKX	NC	6	16 7	62	DD
1927	BKX	NC	6	18 6	70	DD
1927	BKX	NC	6	19 1½	74	DD
					or 39	SD
1927	BKX	NC	6	16 5	62	DD

also available as forward control FBKX models a 4-cylinder version was also offered known as FBX the w/b of this chassis was probably 16ft 5in

Year	Model	Control	Wheels	W/B ft in	Seats	SD or DD
1926	OWD	NC	4	11 6	16	SD
1927	OWD	NC	4	12 5	20	SD
1929	OND	NC	4	12 5	20	SD
1929	ONDF	FC	4	12 5	20	SD
1932	ONDL	NC	4	Longer than above	More than above	SD
1933	CF14	NC	4	10 6	14	SD
1933	CF20	NC	4	12 6	20	SD
1934	Vixen 24	NC	4	12 6	24	SD
1934	Vixen 26	NC	4	14 9	26	SD

The above were made in small numbers until 1940

Year	Model	Control	Wheels	W/B ft in	Seats	SD or DD
1933	FD32	FC	4	16 7½	32	SD
1933	FD48	FC	4	16 7½	48	DD
1933	FD35	FC	4	27 6	35	SD
1933	FDX60	FC	6	-	60	DD

The last FD32s were purchased by Burton on Trent in 1940-41.

WARTIME AND POST-WAR GUY BUSES

Year	Model	Control	Wheels	WB ft in	Seats	DD or SD
1942	Arab Mk1	Forward	4	16 3	56	DD
1943	Arab Mk2	Forward	4	16 3	56	DD

(chassis lengthened by 5 in to 26ft 5in)

Year	Model	Control	Wheels	WB ft in	Seats	DD or SD
1946	Arab Mk3	Forward	4		41	SD
1947	Arab Mk3	Forward	4			DD
1947	Wolf	NC	4		20	SD
1947	Vixen	Forward	4		30	SD
1950	Arab UF	Forward	4		40	SD
1950	Otter LLOB	Forward	4		30	SD
1951	Arab IV	Forward	4		54	DD
1952	Arab LUF	Forward	4		37	SD
1954	NLLVP (GS)	Normal	4		26	SD
1956	Warrior	Forward	4		64	SD
1958	Wulfrunian	Forward	4		75	DD
1959	Victory	Forward	4			SD
1959	Seal	Forward	4		24	SD
1962	Arab V	Forward	4			DD
1975	Victory	Forward	4			DD
1978	Victory II	Forward	4			DD

APPENDIX THREE
Military vehicle production 1923-1945

Date Production Commenced	Description
c1923	Guy 30 cwt 4x2 supplied to Army and Royal Navy.
c1924-25	Guy 30 cwt Roadless half-track. Six to Army, at least one mounting water tank body. Two civilian examples also took in an expedition around the north of Australia.
c1926-28	Guy BAX and FBAX 3 ton 6x4 subsidy types. Extensive range of bodies for military purposes.
1930	Guy Light/Medium six-wheeler was tested by the army as an alternative to the subsidy type. It did not catch on and even Bovington Museum has no further information on this model.
c1931	Guy 6x6 and 8x8 experimental artillery tractors tested in UK; external drive line. A 6x4 version, the CAX, was supplied in some numbers to India and later a similar chassis was used for a big Indian armoured car, body by Vickers.
c1936-38	Guy Demon scout car. Prototype only, 4x2, very unusual. Guy Ant and Quad Ant in various forms. Guy Armoured Car Marks I & IA. Originally known as the Wheeled Tank, eventually gained the company an award for welding armour plate. Production moved to Karrier in the war but Guy supplied some armoured bodies. Some vehicles were badged as Humber, none as Karrier.
1937-38	Guy Lizard 4x4 3 ton; two prototypes believed built for Army.
c1939-40	Guy wheeled carrier. In effect a wheeled version (4x4) of the tracked Universal (Bren) Carrier, few details available.
c1939	Guy Otter based petrol-electric vehicle for searchlights.
1940-41	Guy Lizard Armoured Command vehicle; some 21 built and used in UK and Middle East. Later developed by AEC but Guy seemed to have built the prototype bopies.

GUY MOTORS IN RETROSPECT

The following pages include extracts from a selection of letters received in response to an appeal for information published in the *Wolverhampton Star*. They convey, sometimes quite poignantly, how the workforce who made the company what it was, went about their daily working lives. For many those were 'the best years of their lives'.

From Mr C. J. Jones

I write to say that although now in my 94th year, on leaving school in 1918 I volunteered for Army Service and on leaving the Army in 1919, at a time when thousands of men with work experience were pouring out of the army, whilst I had no experience whatever I considered myself fortunate to obtain my first job at Guy Motors. I was appointed as a clerk to the manager of the materials test department under a Mr S. Hervins, the work mainly being reports on various tests.

I became interested in the machines operated in the Dept., small centre lathes, large capstan centre lathes, milling and drilling machines and in the preparation for Tensile, Fracture and Impact tests of the various materials, before and after hardening. After hardening the fracture pieces were ground down to a thickness of about ½in, when further tests were made and then drillings were taken from the hardened core for the Chemist Analyst.

I also had the pleasure of playing football for Guy Motors F. C. in the Wolverhampton & District League.

I can confirm that I was very happy working there in good conditions. You may not be aware that in addition to the excellent motor lorries, coaches etc Guys also produced a small number of saloon Motor Cars known as Model F, one of which was used regularly by Managing Director, Mr Sydney Guy.

So I worked at Guy's in 1919 and 1920. When the Government released thousands of army lorries in late 1919, many unused, on to the market it hit many lorry manufacturers very hard. Guy Motors immediately sacked the night shift of about 1,200 men at two hours notice, followed a week or two later by the decimation of the day shift, including myself, again at two hours notice.

* Mr Jones later joined the Inland Revenue Dept and retired in 1965 as one of H. M. Inspectors of Taxes.

From Miss Pat Williams

My Grandfather Mr Sam Halford didn't work for Guy's but he was the umpire for their cricket team for many years.....

When he decided to 'retire' from being umpire because at 82 years of age he thought he was getting too old, the cricket team presented him with a wrist watch of which he was very proud, and he wore it until he died at the age of 94.

From Mrs M. Maybury

My late husband, J. C. Maybury, was an ex-Sunbeam apprentice in the 1930s. He worked for Guy Motors for 45 years 'till he retired on the day he was 65. Twelve months later Guy Motors closed down with full order books, a handsome profit and a good work force.

It was a happy place to work, not very good pay but plenty of jokes and laughter. He was a planner in the Experimental shop, later taking the Management course at Malvern and made Staff status as a Foreman. As he said, you had to wait for dead men's shoes.

It was a shame it closed but Wolverhampton has lost so many of its factories which kept its population in work.

Sydney Guy the founder was very much liked and treated all his work force as family. There have been several get togethers of recent years but sadly Jack is no longer with us.

From Mrs G. Pryce

For 16 years 1950/1966 I was the M.D.'s secretary, working for Mr Sydney S. Guy who was chairman as well as M.D., and for Mr A. G. Jones his successor.

I enjoyed those years when I was known as "Mrs Van" prior to my second marriage. Mr Guy was a wonderful personality and he had his own brand of charm. A hard taskmaster, but fair. Nothing annoyed him more than someone lying to cover up an error.

At the same time his record was inspiring, the sacrifices he made to keep the firm afloat in difficult times. He worked tremendously hard himself and looked for the same quality in those around him.

Social evening at Guymo Club 1954. Right to left: Mrs G. Pryce, Rex Jones, Joyce Nicholls, Mrs Fawdrey, David Griffiths and Sylvia Perkins.

GUY MOTORS IN RETROSPECT

From Mr Fred Berry:

When the 1918 armistice came I was only eleven, but I have been informed that Sydney Guy sent the workers home for the day, and the second day he sent them home again. On the third day a party had been organised, during which Sydney listed the Works part in the war work: so many depth charges, so many radial plant engines, (when I worked at Guys there was one of those engines mounted on a wall in the engine test house) and so many cigarette lighters, of course made from bullet cases by the smokers.

I left school at 14 in 1921 and started at Guy Motors as a 'Dog's Body' to Mr Buckerfield the machine shop superintendent. He used to wax the ends of his moustache and was nicknamed "Horns of Bonigale", after a local pub. Not long after I started work, there was a pageant at Tewkesbury Abbey. Someone organised an outing to go there, Sydney came with us. 'Charabang' to Worcester, then by boat to Tewkesbury. We had a good time.

I soon moved to the machine shop, cutting the cotter slot in engine valves (½d each, piece work). It was the duty of a man named Miller to look after the young, he was very kind. The snag was, he was a very broad Scotsman.

I was allowed two afternoons a week at Technical College. About 1924 the government issued a specification for what they called a subsidy commercial vehicle. It was to be of 50-60 cwt capacity. To qualify for the Government subsidy it had to be no more in unladen weight than the specification stated. Guys had difficulty in getting the weight down. They had to drill quite large holes through each crank throw, and right through the camshaft. To further save weight the engine crank case and sump were made of metal which looked like aluminium but was only two-thirds of the weight of aluminium. I have seen fine swarf catch fire if a little sand in the metal created a spark in the fine swarf, whilst taking a finished cut.

In 1929 I moved into the Drawing Office as a junior draughtsman. The Chief Design Engineer was J. D. Buckney, he had his own private office. He became Chief of Wheeled Vehicles Design at the Ministry of Defence. I was handed over to a senior designer who was working on the design of the world's first 8-wheel drive, 4-wheeled steering vehicle for the Defence Ministry. It was tested towing a 19 ton gun in the Welsh Mountains. The Japs came and had a look.

The Chief Draughtsman was W. Gilbert. His assistant was L. K. Andrews. One afternoon he was missing for a long spell, when he did return, he pinned a notice on the office door which stated that Mr Guy had just appointed him as Chief Designer ! W. Gilbert joined us reading the notice. Andrews did not stay long and became an agent for Motor Units etc. He later joined Vulcan Motors Southport where he was killed test driving a vehicle.

I do remember Guys sued the War Office re 150 armoured car chassis which were intended for the India Office, the chassis were all completed, and were parked all over the place, because the War Office changed the axle ratio, and after that they decided that they wanted a circular radiator, built round the fan, very expensive !

Sydney engaged Sir John Simon whose fee alone came to £19,000. It was finally settled out of court. Guys received £30,000, and another big order several months later. I remember it well, we had to run a night shift in the D.O. producing blue prints for the court the next day. I remember the particular Sunday, it was the day when the airship R.34 was destroyed.

Come the slump of the 'thirties, there were 31 of us in the drawing office, and the date was 1931. Slowly orders dwindled, by September that year we didn't have a job between us, we chattered and read the papers and did the same on Saturday 9 am to noon.

Bill Gilbert went missing on this particular Saturday morning, but he came back at 11.50 am with 29 Notices, the remaining two were kept on, hoping for work to come in.

Towards my last year (1930/31) Guys were considering the diesel engine for trucks and buses. I had the honour of doing the installation drawings for the first diesel engined Guy vehicle, it was a Gardner 6-cylinder originally designed for marine purposes. It weighed 17 cwt. Gardner eventually got the weight to 11 cwt.

Publicity Dept thought up an aluminium American Indian's head. The casting was complete with feathered head dress bearing the names of important clients of Guys. The logo was 'feathers in our cap'. This was meant to be mounted on the radiator cap. Some of the wags used to say the feathers should be placed elsewhere !

Guy Motors Gleemen were a singing group of men. About once a month they would give a free concert in the Victoria Hotel which was the top hotel in Wolverhampton.

Again when I worked there Algernon Webb was Sales Director. If he was expecting important visitors he always wore a cravat and tail coat and striped trousers.

Sydney Guy bought the Star Car Works but did not manage to put it on its feet again. Guys made a big car, I think it was in the twenties. Its lines were far in advance of any others in the market and it had an attractive real copper radiator. In shape it was very much like a Rolls Royce except that the front was not flat, the centre vertical was a little forward of the edges of the radiator.

You may be aware that Sydney Guy was Works Manager at Sunbeam Cars at the age of 25, so it was only natural for him to prowl round his own factory, and it was not unknown for him to watch a workman, then borrow the man's smock and show him how to do the job.

Knowing his work force was natural to him. I think my father, F. H. Berry, who was a machinist, was very well liked by Sydney Guy because he was level headed and took the heat out of an argument. Once in particular father stood on a heap of castings in the yard and talked the hot heads down.

My dad was chosen to present a silver salver to Sydney to mark the 25th year of Guy Motors.

When my dad was in hospital Sydney wrote a letter to him by hand and had it delivered to him direct.

The sand blast plant was a totally enclosed metal room with a long bench inside. The operator worked inside protected by helmet and clothing and head gear not unlike a diver, with an air pipe to the outside.

The rate fixer was not a popular man, someone painted 'Ratefixers Strong Room' on the door.

On the whole I would say that Sydney was very proud of the workforce, who had a lot of respect for him. Sometimes when he was in his office he would come through on his 'tannoy' system, and start off by saying, "Listen to me chaps".

I think he regarded us all as part of his team.

GUY MOTORS IN RETROSPECT

From Joyce Calverley:

I worked for Guy Motors at Fallings Park for several years in the Drawing Office. I was a Tracer along with three or four others, seventeen years old. I also operated a very old fashioned blue print machine, with the Arc lamps in an adjacent office.

I remember the first year we were given a Xmas bonus, it must have been around 1935. They were a good firm to work for. I liked my job.

* Note: Mrs Calverley husband was one of the men responsible for the design of the armoured car.

Guy all-welded armoured car outside the War Office. From left to right: Lord Chief Justice Cohen, Mr Bullock, technical director and Mr Southall, solicitor.

The late Alf Parkes at work in the cab track fitting shop in 1974. Alf started working for Guys at the age of fourteen in the late 'twenties and is seen assembling the interior trim on a Big J cab.

From: Terry Greenwood:

Each year on Christmas Eve, remember in those days it was two days off and you worked to the very last on Christmas Eve, at two o'clock all the employees would gather in the canteen to listen to Sydney Guy's Christmas Message. Always, he concluded with,

"I do not pay a Christmas bonus as I know that each time the bell sounds for knocking off time I lose the equivalent of one complete bus chassis and I consider this to be an all year bonus. You may leave work if you wish to do so to get your last minute shopping but please remember to clock out"

From Kathleen Thomas:

Major H. S. McTyer, the company secretary, was the owner of an Armstrong Siddley car. The story goes that one Saturday lunchtime he was in the act of buying shoes at Barker's shoe shop in Lichfield Street, Wolverhampton when, whilst he was looking in the window, he saw the reflection of his car slowly moving from the parking place outside. He rushed outside hoping he was going to stop it by placing himself in front of it. Imagine his embarrassment when he looked up and saw a bewildered driver - his own car, being identical, was parked behind just as he had left it.

Devotion to Duty - James A. Stanley

Fred Baxter, a rather rough and ready rogue and a foreman in the bottom body shop was working on a high-sided van of a scaffold arrangement.

He stepped back to admire his work.

On rising from the ground after a 10ft drop,

he shook himself and climbed back up to finish the job.

Such devotion to duty !

"THAT'S THAT HORRID MAN PLAYING WITH HIS LEVELLING VALVE AGAIN!"

DRAWING OFFICE
DINNER
1959

The drawing office personnel held their annual dinner in a Wolverhampton hotel each Christmas and produced a suitable programme. The wags in the department could be relied upon to bring a smile to all concerned and one of the covers, right, shows a hitherto little-known virtue of the Wulfrunian's air suspension system's levelling valves.

GUY MOTORS IN RETROSPECT

Ron Thomas built several models for the company, one of which is seen, above, in the foyer of the front offfice and below, in close-up. One of Ron's models of the South African factory is also shown opposite. At the time of going to press he was busy making a half-scale model of a Rolls Royce motor car.

GUY MOTORS IN RETROSPECT

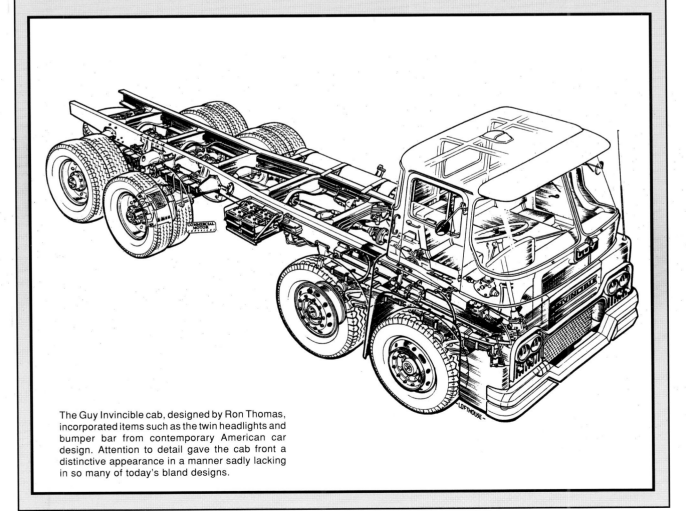

The Guy Invincible cab, designed by Ron Thomas, incorporated items such as the twin headlights and bumper bar from contemporary American car design. Attention to detail gave the cab front a distinctive appearance in a manner sadly lacking in so many of today's bland designs.

From R. L. Waterhouse

I worked for Guy Motors for 8½ years. I was a chargehand in the Matlin Stores Hanger which was used to house major items.

My job was to keep different sections of track building supplied at all times.

I took a great interest not only in day to day things but in Guys itself.

It was one big happy family, a way of life you felt proud to be part of. We worked as a team at Guys and the quality of the products was second to none.

I believe myself that at the time Leyland's idea was to buy and close old names and reduce the competition. Why close a profitable plant with a full order book. Nobody will change my mind that it was not political. I lost a house through it; it makes me angry.

Going on to the good times, it was like a time warp to see the old vehicles stored in the top yard.

There was a rumour that at the end of the war when there was a surplus of war vehicles and because top yard was only hard-core and wanted building up, vehicles were buried under it.

At Guy we built the prototype Land-Train which was used in the Yorkie-Bar advert.

I shall never forget the day in 1982 we had the kiss of death from Old King Dole.

I was called to the board room with other shop stewards and the convener. I was a Transport & General Workers Union steward over the Storemen and Drivers.

Michael Edwards sat opposite me and said the plant was closing, it was like a bomb going off. British Leyland claimed it would cost too much to bring the factory up to date.

During working to the shut down of the plant I was one of seven loading stock to go to Leyland, other things were auctioned off for pennies to different buyers. I was one of the last to go in October 1982 when the gates were shut for the last time.

Most employees went around August and just after. Companies went bust over it, orders were cancelled when firms found out that Guys were not building them any more. At the time I said to foreman Alan Jones "I bet Sydney Guy is turning in his grave at this lot."

Guy used fibreglass in buses and lorries, but it is less well-known that they also made fibreglass swimming pools, and bodies for the Frisky car which was developed by Meadows. Who tested the swimming pools in the factory is not recorded.

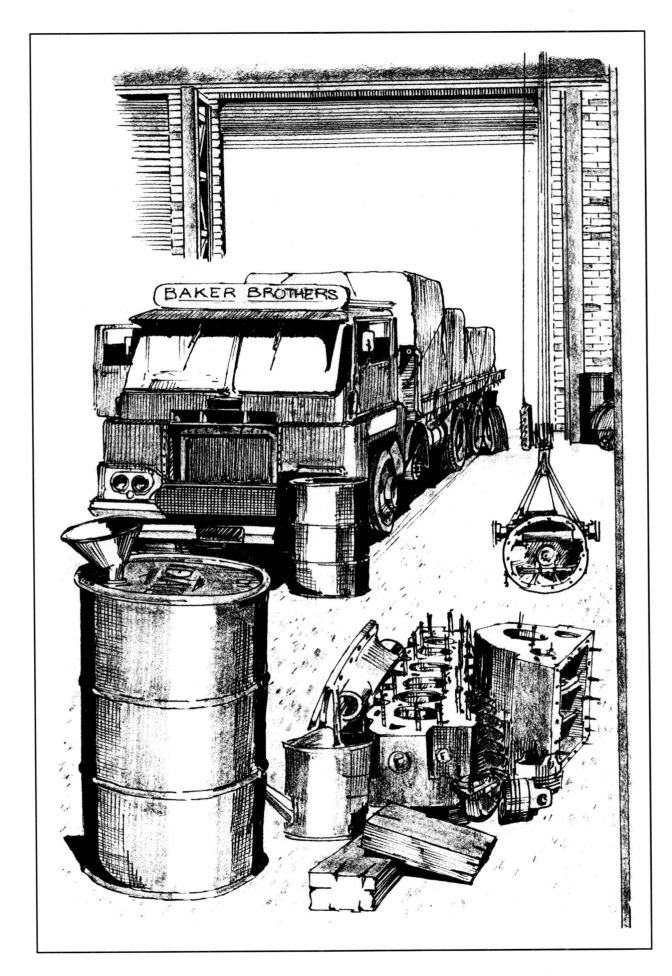

Owning a restored Guy vehicle can give a lot of pleasure. Spare parts are not always easy to obtain, but the quality of the engineering is high and reliability excellent, once the vehicle is restored.

The Guy owners club is worth joining even if you just have an interest in the marque.

The club is run by Ron Lucas who worked for Guy Motors for a number of years. The annual fee is £10 (£7.50 for ex-employees), members receive a newsletter and regular meetings are held in the Wolverhampton area.

Once a year owners of old Guy vehicles take part on a rally organised by the club.

Guy Owners Club
120, Dovedale Road
Wolverhampton
WV4 6RB

Insurance for your restored Guy can be arranged through:

Trevor Keef, Footman James Co Ltd
Waterfall Lane
Cradley Heath
West Midlands

ADC 802	19
AEC	45, 114
AEC Q	75
Air Suspension	90
Albion Motors	114
American Indian	76
Armoured Car	51
Australian Government	32
Automatic Chassis Lubrication	11
Barton, T. H.	37
Bedford	43, 45, 57
Belfast Corporation	**68**
Bellis & Morcom	9
Betjeman, J.	17
Birgward, C.	76
Birkenhead Corporation	**122**
Birmingham City Transport	**28**, **36**, **37**, **70**, 126, **126**
Black, W	125
Blackburn Corporation	**122**
Blackpool Corporation	34
Boally	**102, 106**
Bournemouth Corporation	17, 64, **64**, **127**
Britain's First Six-Wheel Bus	27
British Motor Corporation	114
Bristol	57
Brockway	9
Brown, David	90, 110, 113
Buckney, E.D.	11
Buick	9
Burlingham	90
Burton-on-Trent Corporation	19, 44, **66**
Bus Grant	128
BUSAF	117
Cadillac	11, 92
Chester Cocporation	117, **118**, **122**, **128**
Chevrolet	45
Chrysler	114
Chrysler, W.	12
Chrysler Model B	12
Commer	75
Commercial Motor	90, 97, 110
Commercial Motor Show	81, 90, 102, 106, 110, 117
Cotal	45
County Motors	**100**
Courtaulds	57
Cox, E	86
Cromwell Tank	57
Crusader Tank	55
Cummins	104, 110
Daimler-Knight	19, 24, 32
Daimler	19, 37, 57, 102, 110, 114
Darlington Corporation	29
Dennis Brothers	35
Derby Corporation	41
Dodge Trucks	113
Dodson	29
Dorman-Ricardo	43
East Kent Road Car Co	**121**
East Lancashire	97
Eastern Coach Works	76
Edinburgh Corporation	**123, 125**
Electric Construction Co, The	31
Elliott, C.	113
ENV	113
ERF	76
Evans, P. J.	9
Express Motors	35

Fageal, F. & W.	75
Fallings Park	110, 86
Firestone	92
Foden	110
Ford	45, 114
Fuller	90
Gardner	19, 36, 37, 45, 57, 66, 70, 75, 76, 90, 92, 97, 110
General Motors	37, 90, 92
German Army	51
Girling	97
GMC Type 4104	
Goliath Werke GMbH	76
Great War	10
Greyhound	90
Guy	45, 55
Guy 13/36	**12, 13**
Guy 12 hp	12
Guy 16.9 hp	12
Guy 15 cwt	**40**
Guy 30 cwt	14, **17** Guy 30 cwt 14, **17**
Guy 2 ton	**40**
Guy 2/3 ton Battery Electric	**17**
Guy 2 ton chassis	14
Guy 3-axle chassis	**27**
Guy advertisement	**33, 49, 50**
Guy Ambulance	23
Guy Ant	45, 46, 51, **59**
Guy Arab	**47**, **54**, 55, **55**, 57, 71, **71**, **71**, **87**, **121**, **125**
Guy Arab (Utility) Cab	**61**
Guy 1000th Arab (Utility) chassis	**63**
Guy Arab II	**122**
Guy Arab III	**68**, 70, **70**, **73**, **123**
Guy Arab IV	70, **101**, **118**, **128**
Guy Arab V	**100**, **101**, 117, **118**, **128**
Guy Arab, Last	117, **128**
Guy Armoured Car	**52**
Guy Army Trials	45
Guy B	18, 19
Guy BA	18, 19
Guy BB	19, **20**, 23, **53**
Guy BB 3 ton	**21**
Guy BT	**31**, **41**, **48**, 51, **68**
Guy BTX	**41**, **48**, 51, **56**
Guy BTX Demonstrator	31
Guy BTX Trolleybus	**30, 31**
Guy Big J	**103**, **104**, **105**, **106**, **107**, **108**, **109**, 113, **115**, **116**
Guy C Range	34
Guy Charabanc	14, **15**
Guy Conquest	**36**
Guy Gas Producer truck	**32**
Guy Goliath	76, **80**
Guy GS	**126**
Guy Horsebox	**21**
Guy Invincible	37, 43, **80**, **81**
Guy Invincible II	**82**, **83**, **84**, 87, 90, **90**, **91**, 97
Guy J	**18**, **19**, 24
Guy London 6-wheeler bus	**32**
Guy Promenade runabouts	18
Guy Model BAX	27
Guy Model BHX	**28**
Guy Model BX	**27**, 29, 32
Guy Model BTX	**38**, **88**
Guy Model FB	43
Guy Model FBAX	**27**, **45**, **52**
Guy Model FBB	26
Guy Model FBX	32
Guy Model FC	43
Guy Model FCX	**34**, **35**, **36**, **38**

INDEX

Guy Model FC6 Warrior Goliath **39**
Guy Model FCZ **39**
Guy Model FD32 44
Guy Model FD35 44
Guy Model FD48 **43**
Guy Model FDX60 44
Guy Model JA **25**
Guy Model LUF 75, 75
Guy Model O **20**
Guy Model ON **26**
Guy Model PE 45
Guy Model UF 75, **75**
Guy Motor Caravan **20**
Guy Motors 9, 10, 11, 17, 24, 32, 36, 37,
57, 66, 70, 75, 76, 81, 90, 92,
97, 110, 117, 119
Guy Municipal **22**
Guy Production details 130-133
Guy Production Targets **63**
Guy One Tonner **22**
Guy Otter **46**, 70, **72**, 76, **77, 83, 84, 85,**
96, 110, **124, 126**
Guy Otter Mk3 **82**
Guy OWD 31, 34
Guy Owners Club 124, 141
Guy PE 45, 51
Guy Quad 51
Guy R 24
Guy rationalised range 110
Guy Road Rail Vehicle **14, 16**
Guy, Sydney 9, 12, 45, 51, 125
Guy Trolleybus 66, **127**
Guy truck production **16**
Guy truck with Spud wheels **14**
Guy V8 **11, 12,** 17
Guy Victory J 117
Guy Victory 34, 90, 92, **92, 93**
Guy Victory Trambus 117
Guy Vix-Ant 57, 58, 59, **59, 64**
Guy Vixen **50,** 66, **67, 70, 77,** 124
Guy War Department trucks **18**
Guy Warrior 37, 45
Guy Warrior Light 6 **95, 96, 97,** 98
Guy Warrior Light 8 **93,** 98
Guy Warrior MkII **85,** 87, **94**
Guy Warrior (PSV) **98**
Guy Warrior Tractor Unit **93, 96**
Guy Warrior Trambus 117
Guy Wolf **42, 43, 51, 53,** 57, 66, **66, 67,**
71, 81, **121, 124**
Guy Works Committee 24
Guy Wulfrunian 90, 92, **92,** 98, **98, 99,** 110,
128
Guy Wulfrunian Advert **89,** 90,

Harriman, G. 114
Harrods 17
Hart Liddle 51
Haworth, Dr H. F. 24
Hitler Adolf 37
Holden 14
Hong Kong 117
Huddersfield 75
Humber 9
Humber Thomas 9

Jaguar 37, 102, 113, 114
Jennings 15
Johannesburg 119,

Karrier 57, 66
Kingston-upon-Hull 86

Lancashire United Transport **101, 118, 123, 128**
Land Liners 35
Landtrain 117
Leyland 24, 35, 55, 57, 75, 76, 92, 110,
113, 117, 119
Liberty engine 55
Lincoln Corporation **125**
Liverpool Self-Propelled
Traffic Association 17
Llandudno UDC **121, 124, 126**
London Transport **57,** 76, **76, 121**
Lyons, William 99, 102, 110, 113, 114

Mansel, Frank 24
Marathon 117
Markland, S. 114
Marles Steering 43
Mason Bros 32
Massey **122**
McCall White 11
Meadows, Henry 68, 76, 90, 110, 113
Motor Panels
Motor Show 75

National Socialist Party

Owen, Rubery 10

Packard 43, 86
Park Royal 68, 75, 114, 125
Perkins 70, 76
Petrol-electric 29
Phillips, Walter 9
Poppe, Whites 10
Portsmouth Corporation 18
Pressed Steel Company 114

Railing, Harry 9
Receiver 110
Red & White Motor Services 68
Reo Speedwagon 24
Rio de Janerio Tramway 24
Road Traffic Act 1930 43
Rolls Royce 57
Rolls Royce Merlin 55
Rolls Royce Meteor 55
Rootes Group 114
Roosavelt, Franklin D. 37
Rover 114
Royal Agricultural Show 14
Royal Commission on
Awards to Inventors
Royce, Henry 57
Ruston, Hornsby 125, **125**

Saunders 68
Scammell 114
Seddon 110
Sentinel 75
Silvers, Owen 29, 31
South Africa 99, 110, **111, 112,** 117
South African Railways 14
Southampton Corporation **121, 122, 125**
Sunbeam 9, 57, 66, 86
Standard-Triumph 114
Star 45
Star Engineering Co Ltd 24
 Comet 24
 Flyer 24
 Flyer Chassis 25
 Planet 24

INDEX

Star Planet Coupé	45
Steane, J. & A. (Coachbuilders)	17
Stevens, Rees	31
Strachan Brown	32, 35
Studebaker Electric	17
Studebaker, John M	17
S. S. Cars	37
Swallow Sidecar Co	98
Swindon Corporation	**121**
T45	119
Thornycroft	17
TGB Motors	86
Transport, Ministry of	55
Utility buses	55, **55**, 57, **57**, 60, **60**, 61, **61**, 62, **62**, 63, **63**, 65, **65**, **121**, 125, **125**

Vauxhall Motors	12, 24
Wadhams (Coachbuilders)	9
Walker Vehicle Co	17
Walker Model K	17
Wall Street	35
Walsall Corporation	86, **127**
West Bromwich Corporation	34
West Riding Automobile Company	92, **128**
Weston's Cider & Perry	
White	75
Wilson gearbox	45
Wolverhampton Corporation	31, 34, **100**, **101**
Works Council	9
ZF	92

The End